The Accidental Farmer

Adventures of a Serial Entrepreneur

Patti Pokorchak

PPS PUB

PPS Publishing 3-1750 The Queensway Suite 1312 Toronto ON M9C 5H5
www.publisher-ps.com

Ordering Information:
Quantity sales. Special discounts are available on quantity purchases by corporations, associations, and others. For details, contact the publisher at the address above.

Printed in Canada

First Edition
ISBN 978-0-9952750-3-4

Cover Design: Janet Rouss, Get Real Branding
Author Photo on the cover and author bio is by Janet Trost.
Book Deisgn: Doris Chung, Publisher Production Solutions

This book is dedicated to all entrepreneurs and wannabe entrepreneurs.

Following the rules
never got anyone
into a history book.

Don't settle for a normal life
when you can have
an extraordinary one.

Just Do It!

"If I can be a farmer, then you can be any-thing you want to be – as long as you have some basic sales and marketing skills that is!"

Patti Pokorchak, MBA
Serial Entrepreneur

Dear Reader,

Fasten your seatbelts and get ready for the vicarious trip of a lifetime!

Racing from Canada to Europe and back again at a madcap pace, while enjoying all sorts of adventures that only a Patti Pokorchak can encounter.

Having a one-of-a-kind name means having experiences that seem to only happen to me.

Who knew that I would become a:
- Female tech pioneer,
- Leading software expert in Germany,
- Barcode expert,
- Farmer and a
- Sales coach for entrepreneurs.

None of this was ever on my bucket list (especially the farmer bit—hence the title of this book)—but I encourage you to dream big and make those dreams happen. If I can do all of this, so can you.

No one was more afraid than me. No one had less support than me. Somehow I got the guts to go for it at a pretty young age, and I've never let anything stop me from achieving what I want to achieve since.

This is not to say that I haven't failed at things. I've failed often and hard. I liken my life to a roller coaster ride combined with Snakes 'n Ladders. There have been lots of highs and lots of lows, but how will you appreciate the highs if you haven't experienced the lows?

Such is life, and it all balances out in the end to a pretty great one as I count my blessings and not my sorrows daily.

I don't pretend that I have no regrets, but I've made choices and I like the choices I've made.

I've had an interesting life, showing what else you can do with an MBA if you don't climb the corporate ladder but follow your dreams and heart and go for it!

NB: Some names have been changed to protect the innocent and guilty.

TABLE OF CONTENTS

PROLOGUE

....

It was 1980. I was ten feet tall and invincible, the way that most twenty-somethings feel. Failure was not on my radar. I had finished two degrees, despite having vowed at the age of fourteen to never attend university. Working without a degree was way too slow for me to get ahead.

I was ambitious and anxious to climb the corporate ladder, so I put myself through a BComm and an MBA. I always had a feeling that my life would not be typical. Back then, my MBA was a newish degree that I hoped would give me credibility later in life—for once I thought ahead.

I was working for IBM, two and a half years into my second term, selling mainframe computer software. I had achieved membership in the exclusive and coveted IBM 100% club, when I asked myself, **"Is that all there is?"**

To an outside observer I appeared to have everything a person could want—a successful career, doting boyfriend, tons of money, a trendy duplex, sports car, and lots of friends. But

I wasn't happy. There was restlessness within me. I had hoped that there was more to life than this.

In between my two degrees, my parents had gifted me a trip to Europe and it really whetted my appetite for travel around the continent. Since then, it had constantly been in the back of my mind to return for an extended period of time. The beauty of Europe—the culture, people, and history—fascinated me. Now seemed to be the time to return. It really was now or never. And I knew never would be a regret that I would not be able to live with.

I started saving money, paying off my student debts, hiding excess money from myself, so that I wouldn't spend it. Getting promoted into sales at IBM had boosted my income and since my lifestyle was just above a frugal student's one, I was able to save a lot of money.

The decision to leave was a hard one. My choices were: stick with the status quo or enter into the unknown. I could stay at IBM and climb the corporate ladder, marry the boyfriend, and live "happily ever after" OR I could make my dream of travelling in Europe for a year a reality, and see where the future took me. The unknown is a scary place to be for most people and I was no exception.

I had to decide—would I ever be happy staying where I was? Could I live a life with regrets?

They say it takes a traumatic event to make people change. My traumatic event took the form of two weeks away at two IBM conferences with too many groping men. Being a cute young blonde, one of only 100 women in a sea of 5,000 men was not a pleasant experience. This was in the days before sexual harassment was a noted issue and it was barely addressed at all. Women in business were rare then.

At the first conference, I stuck close to my 6'6" guy friend who acted as my bodyguard. Things got ugly the more the guys drank and I did not feel safe by myself.

The second conference was the ultimate goal when working at IBM, called the 100% club, which you were awarded for achieving your target. It was a badge of honour, touted on all promotions. If that was the ultimate goal, then I wanted more, way more in my life.

There had to be more to life than this!

I returned from the trip and waited a week to look respectable, finalized my decision to leave, and resigned. Scary, yes, but my regrets in not going would have been even scarier. I was like that rosebud that Anais Nin wrote about, "And the day came when the risk it took to remain tight in the bud was more painful than the risk it took to blossom".

I sold my meagre worldly possessions, said goodbye to friends and family, and left. A cheap one-way ticket to London was the starting point of my new life as a traveller. Not as a tourist on a short holiday, I was on the adventure of a lifetime. I wasn't drawn to the typical tourist attractions; I wanted to see how the locals lived. I wanted to be a local.

Travelling on my own, I could go wherever I wanted to, whenever I wanted to. I was completely in charge of my life. The freedom was intoxicating. I ended up as far north as Inverness,

Scotland and as far south as Greece and everywhere in between. Although I was technically traveling solo, I met people constantly. I found that I had a great gut instinct for choosing the best places to visit, keeping out of trouble AND for getting lost constantly. This was years before GPS was available, but getting lost was half the fun.

After my year of travel was over, and my money was running out, I realized that I didn't want to return to Toronto. It was too familiar and there was so much more for me to experience in Europe. Having already made the initial decision to leave Toronto and my old life behind, I found it was so much easier to decide to stay for another year. That year of travel taught me so many things that have stayed with me for my whole life.

Most importantly it taught me what absolute freedom looks like. When you have a bit of money in the bank, you can truly do whatever you feel like, whenever you feel like it. To me, that meant buying a car and traveling in fairly decent style. No backpacking or hostels for me (I treasured my privacy after staying in one hostel and not sleeping all night).

Having a Canadian passport also gave me freedom that others who were born in Communist countries did not have. It's something that we Westerners take for granted, until you meet someone your own age that does not have the same privileges as you do, just because of where they were born. I just didn't know how lucky I was. I've never taken my Canadian citizenship and freedom for granted since then.

I also learned how resilient I could be, as I managed to get myself through multiple car troubles in countries where I had no language skills— whether that meant flagging down a truck driver in small town Hungary and miming my problem or getting a group of guys to push start my car in Budapest. I learned how to navigate in places where the road ended and I was thoroughly lost. The kindness of strangers has never lost its magic for me.

Although I had heard German spoken all my life, I had only started speaking it that year and my language skills were still fairly basic. Learning how to respond to job ads in German was an interesting experience. They wanted a photo of you and transcripts of all your education, even your elementary and high school certificates; plus, reference letters from all employers and copies of your actual degrees.

That forced me to finally tell my parents that I had been kicked out of my MBA school (you'll get those sordid details later) as my credentials and the letter expelling me were in the same folder that my parents had to send to me from home.

As I was in a rush to find a job and a place to live, I decided to do a "Work Wanted" ad in the big weekend edition newspaper. I got a few inquiries but the most promising came from a small start-up software company who hired me. They thought they had struck gold finding me with my IBM background. I just wanted to live and work in a foreign country and was willing to settle for any job that would let me break even while living in Munich. You'll read more about those adventures later in the book.

So are you waking up wondering if this is all there is for you?

You could be like most entrepreneurs and never "work" a day in your life because work is such a joy… Okay, so most of us entrepreneurs work too much but it's because we truly love what we do and don't consider it work. Think about it, do you often hear many entrepreneurs complaining about their "jobs"? There is a lot of truth in the quote, "Entrepreneurship is living a few years of your life like most people won't so that you can spend the rest of your life like most people can't".

The main difference between those who love their life and those who plod through life bitter and bemoaning their lot, is that the lovers of life don't settle. They take personal responsibility for where they are and for where they are going. I've been tied to a hated job because of debt and it's not a pleasant place to be.

In my mind, you only regret your age if you're not living a happy and fulfilled life, rich with adventures and rewarding deeds. To remedy this, you don't necessarily have to run away for a year like I did, but it might involve stepping out of your comfort zone and trying something new. If all you ever do are the same things, there's no surprise as to why you're bored and unhappy.

Stepping outside your comfort zone can involve little things too. For some, that might mean going to a movie or eating out by yourself—learning to be happy alone. For others, that might mean climbing Kilimanjaro or going on a solo trip. I've travelled for 35 years on my own and it definitely has its rewards.

With Meetup groups and other networking sites, you never have to be truly alone when you try something new. There's a group for every interest out there from kayaking to improv to quilting.

Getting out of your comfort zone is just like using a muscle that you haven't exercised for a while. It will hurt like heck the first time you work it, but with continual use it gets stronger, more flexible and you will be able to bend it to your will. For me, the ache of staying and living a life with regrets, was greater that the risk of leaving it all behind for an adventure. I'm happy to say that I have no regrets in my life.

CITY SLICKER VEGGIES

....

FINDING THE RIGHT MARKET

I n 2000 I moved out to the country to live with my (then future, now ex) husband. My dislike of commuting to the city of Ottawa and being burnt out after twenty-five years of working in high tech made me look around at my new rural home and wonder what I could do with it. I couldn't envision not working. It just wasn't in the cards for me to slow down, and just enjoy life. I was way too young to even consider that as an option.

I had a growing interest in plants, a green thumb, one eight-week class on perennials and eight acres to play with, so why not start my own garden centre? Was it a sound basis for a new business? Not quite. It's not something that I, as a sales, marketing and business coach, would have ever recommended to a client; but then again, what consultant ever takes their own advice?

Right after our honeymoon, the first trip taken with my new husband (word of advice: go on holidays before you get married to see how compatible you are), I started Down to Earth Gardens. The fact that I had no formal education in horticulture, no desire to work in retail and, above all, thought that anything to do with Mother Nature was stupid, was not stopping me.

The winter before opening, I spent hours researching how to run a greenhouse and garden centre.. The usual advice was to work in a garden centre first. Well that wasn't happening as I was planning to open mine that spring. Reading about farming can only get you so far and I knew I was just going to have to do my best and learn on the job, as I had done so often in the past.

Not having done something before has never been a stopper for me and shouldn't be for you either.

There is always a first time for everyone. No one starts out knowing what they know now.

Needless to say, my first summer running the garden centre was a huge learning experience, as well as a total shock to my body and mind. I'd get up before dawn, as light was just beginning to show over the horizon. I was so excited about what I was going to learn and do every day; it was all so new and challenging. It was such a change to start washing up at the end of my workday instead of at the start and putting on casual work clothes instead of suits and dresses. I loved it.

To turn this farm into what a garden centre should look like, I first needed to tackle my long, barren driveway. It was the first thing visitors would see driving in and I needed it to look lush and inviting. Although I was impatient, there were some things I couldn't make happen before their time. It takes three years for a perennial plant to mature. No amount of begging or pleading will make any iota of difference. Mother Nature demands her time and the farm didn't look like a gardening oasis until my third year in business. I had many heartbreaking episodes of watching cars drive in, turn around, and drive back out without stopping because the plants and display gardens were well-hidden behind our oversized garage and trees.

I started planting a variety of things in my driveway beds to see what would survive and tried desperately to fill up a space that needed about 1,000 plants to look even somewhat landscaped. My two "flowerbeds" were 250 feet long by 8 feet wide and I had no idea how much time and effort it would take to plant and weed that space.

What was I thinking? Well I wasn't. It was a good thing in the end as it turned out to be an amazing entrance to my garden centre…eventually.

I had no idea about the amount of work those beds would be. But I had a vision. I planted 250 sunflower seeds. Do you know how much hard work it is to get rid of those sunflowers the next year? They have massive roots and you have to pull them all up before you can plant new ones—just one of the consequences of not knowing what to plant and where. BUT they did look spectacular and that was part of my vision.

I had seeds for a type of ornamental corn and decided to plant a few rows of that in the driveway as well. In mid-August, as I was admiring the pretty six-foot-tall corn stalks with their tri-coloured leaves and multi-coloured cobs, it suddenly dawned on me—you're in the country now, no one grows "pretty" veggies here! It's either cattle corn or human corn. Pretty corn? No way!

Only a confirmed city slicker would grow that. My pride turned to shame. I saved the seeds anyways to grow again, as I knew a market would be there, I only had to figure out where that market was.

That led me to realize that Down to Earth Gardens served two very distinct markets:

My rural clientele. These customers would be the first to ask what vegetable plants I had. They were interested in useful plants and not wildflowers and ornamental grasses (which they considered to be weeds—"you charge money for that?"). They would also ask for beneficial companion plants, those that attracted the right insects or deterred the wrong ones.

My urban customers. Those from surrounding cities would immediately ask for "those popular ornamental grasses everyone is raving about". They were also interested in the pretty yellow wildflowers growing in my garden (aka Goldenrod). I was embarrassed to note that it was an unplanted-by-me flower, a weed.

I discovered that this same yellow plant (Goldenrod) could either be an unwanted weed or a treasured gem, depending on where you lived and how you looked at it.

Perspective is everything isn't it?

From a business point of view, you have to know who your ideal market is or be able to segment them appropriately and have something for each one. In my case, I usually just looked at their car and clothes, asked a few questions about the size of their garden and could determine if they were rural or city folks.

My garden centre was only one long country mile around the corner from a high-end and well-established nursery. Their display gardens had been there for over twenty-five years, and were lush and well kept. My newly planted gardens really showed their immaturity as it takes time for plants to grow—hence the need for the 250 sunflowers, which are notorious for being fast growers.

Our two markets sometimes intersected but at most times were distinctly our own. We were literally as different as night and day, as they had quite a shady spot that specialized in shade plants and larger exotic trees and my hot and sunny farm dealt with smaller starter plants. Also, where my prices stopped—theirs started.

The other nursery's owners, "the boys" as I called them, were knowledgeable gardeners and landscape designers who had been working their own gardens for decades. I was barely beyond the novice stage of gardening and was only beginning to tackle my first major design project.

So how was I going to stand out from the more experienced garden centre around the corner from me? With my lack of experience, but keen desire to learn more about plants, I figured there had to be a lot of other clueless gardeners out there for me to cater to. That's when I came up with my tag line of "Easy care plants for novice, busy and black thumb gardeners". Welcome to the home of the "unkillable" plant! That pretty much covered everyone except for "plant snobs" who would not like my plants, prices or property.

It was rural gardening gone wild! It drove my OCD husband nuts, but my customers and I loved it. Cars would crawl up the driveway, their passengers looking left and right as the birds and butterflies flitted around the plants. If you liked tidy, manicured gardens, where you could see soil between plants, this was not your place. But if you loved colours and plants that thrived with healthy neglect, then this was your haven.

I learned so much from books, my own hands-on experience and from my customers in the first few years. My sales technique of asking lots of questions came in handy for learning what grew where and how. I found that if I knew a few basic things about someone's garden, I could recommend the right plant for their place. If a plant was trendy but fussy, I let people know.

I found that if I could tell people stories of how I came to grow that particular plant, where it was best suited for, its quirks and characteristics, I could help to make their choices safe and easy. I enabled people to go from bare soil to blooms in one season, without any gardening knowledge or experience.

Since I had already experienced all the wrong things to plant—like invasive plants that take over your lawn (garden thugs, they were called)—I came up with strategies, like planting two thugs together and letting them duke it out. That way they were both kept in line, and many thugs are really nice plants when kept under control. Pruning them heavily in the springtime was also key to keeping them in check.

What I learned was that by focusing my business on a fairly large but targeted group of gardeners, I made my garden a destination for the horticulturally challenged. It was a safe place for them to come and ask any gardening question. I would put together plant groups for them, showing them what would go well together in their space. I'd draft up a quick sketch of what to plant and where and they'd be on their way after leaving their folding green stuff behind with me.

Once you find your niche, your "people", your "peeps', your "tribe", it makes your business and marketing that much easier. It's so much more efficient and economical to target a smaller group of prospects and speak their language, like a sharpshooter, rather than using the shotgun approach of targeting everyone and no one at the same time.

It became obvious that I could never persuade a rural resident to buy an ornamental variant of a crop that they raised for their livestock, much less persuade a "plant snob" to go for my cheap, easy-care shrubs that were not the latest variety in the gardening magazines. This knowledge of my market allowed me to really hone in on my customer's needs and cater my sales approach to every individual.

In turn, my garden sales grew by word-of-mouth referrals and returning customers bringing along their friends. Down to Earth Gardens became one of the go-to places on the spring garden centre tours, proving that it pays to know your customer well.

Whose problem or pain do you solve the best and the easiest?

You might be too in love with your own products to really see who will benefit the most from it. It's not always obvious who your target market is and why they might benefit from your product. Don't assume anything and hit them across the head with why they need what you're offering. Likewise, you shouldn't try to be too clever or subtle either and miss getting your message across.

There is no substitute for being 100% clear on what the benefits of your products are and who can benefit the most from it. You can take the same product, tweak your message and target market and either have a runaway success or a dismal failure.

Should you have a marketing fail, it doesn't mean that you should throw your product away—it might just mean that you had the wrong target, wrong focus or wrong message or a combination of all three things. Try again and keep trying until you succeed. It really is a matter of getting the right message for the right product in front of the right target client.

I get really riled up when I talk about marketing initiatives and someone says, "I've tried that already and it doesn't work". Does a baby learn to walk in one easy go? Did you learn to ride a bicycle on your first attempt?

So, why should you think that you could master marketing the first time you try? The fact that they tried a new marketing initiative once, failed, and never tried again does not mean that it will never work for them. It just means that they have to try a new way and keep trying until it does.

Thomas Edison said that his first 3,000 filaments were not failures, but served to let him know what didn't work. The same thing goes with your marketing. Don't expect to have a bestseller or to go 'viral' right from the start.

There are few overnight successes but most of us plod along, going two steps forward and one step back until we've made it. FYI: most "overnight successes" take at least 10-20 years to happen.

So what does your typical client look like?
What is their sex, age and profession?
Where do they live?
What books and magazines do they read?
What TV programs do they watch?
What social media channels are they active on?

The more you know about your target market, the easier it becomes to create a marketing message that will get them interested and attract their attention.

Try, try and try again. In marketing, there is a lot of trial and error. While marketing is what I call an inexact science, there are some scientific principles that can be applied to marketing projects. For example, if you're sending out an email campaign; the most crucial part is the subject line.

That is something that you are able to test. With your target market in mind, you can come up with a multitude of different subject lines. Then you can take a section of your mailing list—say, batches of one hundred names and test two to three different subject lines and track which one gets the most opens and clicks. It's that simple.

When starting your own business, make sure you know whom you are targeting and that "everyone" is NOT a target.

Remember that one person's weed can be another's treasured plant. Narrow it down as finely as you can and you'll be seen as the expert in that niche. You can always expand that niche but you cannot market to the world unless you're a billionaire. And if you are a billionaire, you're probably not reading this book for business advice!

PIONEER PATTI

....

BREAKING INTO NEW MARKETS

A pioneer is defined as a person who is one of the first to use a new method or explore a particular area of knowledge. While prepping for a lecture I was giving at Ryerson University on entrepreneurship and new markets, I realized that I'd spent a large part of my life being a pioneer, usually on the bleeding edge of technology.

I remember playing a golf game on my first computer in 1971, which is why I say that I was born with a computer in my pocket. I was a tech pioneer, being one of the first professional IT females to be hired by IBM.

The second time that I worked at IBM, I sold end-user software on mainframe computers, programs such as word processors and spreadsheets. What we were doing at the time was brand new and had never been sold to that target market before. We found that holding educational seminars for potential clients was the key to success. If people have no idea what you're selling, you have to educate them first and then you can see if there's a need or a fit for them with what you have.

When I was selling and marketing PCs in the early '80s, there was no precedent for selling this kind of technology to consumers. Mainframe computers had mainly been sold to the geeky IT (Information Technology) departments, not end users who had no clue about technology.

Being in a brand new market, our marketing strategy was made up as we went along. We saw what worked and what didn't work and tried to do more of what did work. Again, education was a big part of the business model as sales reps needed to know how the systems worked and where they fit in. Potential clients had to see how the systems could make their business more productive.

When I was working in Europe, I was the software-marketing manager for an American PC manufacturer. I ended up being in the middle of 250 software developers, 200 PC dealers and 75 internal staff members because I was the go-to person for anything software-related. Talk about overload. I didn't need to be quite that popular or overworked. I had to find a way to communicate all the information I gathered in a way that did not involve me as much.

I produced a catalogue that listed all the software that ran on our PCs. Then I threw a huge all-day software fair inviting the dealers and software companies to get together and meet.

By doing so, I was able to stop being the middleman and facilitated new connections and business relationships, which is what really needed to happen in order for hardware to be paired with software. I knew I was doing something right when IBM Germany started copying my marketing efforts.

Fast-forward, to 1992 and I'm back in Canada peddling handheld computers from Psion, a British manufacturer. They designed two products that were identical, except for their exterior and their price.

The Series 3 PDA (Personal Digital Assistant), aka my second brain or e-brain replaced any paper-based organizational system (DayTimer, FiloFax etc.) and cost about $500. It was pricey as compared to the much cheaper paper-based systems out there and came with a learning curve.

The industrial strength computer, the Work-about was meant to be used in warehouses or outside in extreme conditions. This more rugged model was five times more expensive than its counterpart. It took me a while to figure out that it was easier and much more profitable for me to sell a $5,000 asset management system than the $500 personal assistant. Guess who became a barcode expert?

The computers that I worked on continued to get smaller and smaller but the challenges of introducing new technology were still there. In every situation, it really was a matter of educating the potential customers.

An informed prospect buys.

A confused one never does.

Google has made most of our educational requirements a thing of the past. Buyers are now 50-60% certain of their buying decision **before** they contact their short list of preferred suppliers. It's a new world of selling out there.

When breaking into new markets, the most important part is to put yourself into your prospect's shoes and figure out what they need to know in order to be convinced that your product is absolutely necessary to them. More importantly, you'll have to rely on your gut instincts to know how to operate. When you have no role models to follow, you have to make it up as you go along. You have to learn to trust your instincts, which are based on your past experiences and education.

I do not believe that there is an off-the-shelf secret sauce or magic formula that will make you successful. What worked for someone else might not necessarily work for you in your market. But keep trying, you do learn from your mistakes as well as your successes.

The key to starting out as a successful pioneer with a brand new kind of product is to get your first reference account. What you really want are raving fans who are vital in the early stages of a new product introduction. Not many people like the perceived huge risk in being a pioneer; the majority of people like to see that others have made similar decisions before they commit to purchasing.

Getting your first testimonial is what will get you the next client, the one after that and the one after that. It eventually gets easier. Similar to the domino effect, you sell one, and then another and eventually the rest will follow. That is what happened when we first developed our asset tracking systems.

Once we sold to one government department, it was much easier to sell to the next. It's called referral selling ("Don't listen to me but here's what other clients like you did"). Most people do not like being pioneers when it comes to new products. They want to see someone else use it successfully before buying in. Your early adopters have to be handled with kid gloves as they are your entry to future success.

If you're going to give someone a better deal, like a price discount to get them to sign with you, make sure you **ask for something in return**. When you negotiate, never give away something without getting something from your customer. You could ask for personal introductions to three other organizations that could also use your product or a glowing recommendation or review on a public platform like LinkedIn or Yelp. There's no need to cold call if you can get a warm introduction instead. A current satisfied client is worth their weight in gold.

When you've got a revolutionary new product, you have to show how it is better than what is on the market today. People still buy the value that a product has to them. So forget about the features and figure out how they will benefit from your new product or service. People buy outcomes and results; they generally do not care how it happens as long as they gain from it.

Come up with a plan and prioritize, giving top priority to the easiest to do things with the highest payback. Figure out what you have to do to get some reference accounts. Go after the accounts that matter the most to your larger prospect base, as that's where the profit will come.

You don't know if you're going in the wrong direction until you take a step and see if it's right or not. And don't be afraid of starting over if it doesn't work out. Kevin Harrington, from Shark Tank, who has over four billion dollars in sales, stated that two out of three of his products failed. So don't give up until you've given it your best shot.

Needless to say, you also need to know when to give up. You have to be aware of when to hold 'em and when to fold 'em. Playing poker is good training for running a small business. Just make sure that you're not bluffing yourself. Watch Dragon's Den and Shark Tank to get an idea of what you need to do in order to succeed. Ask yourself, "Would investors give me money for this?"

How do you know when your time is running out? Look at your cash flow; however you're financing this business, never take your eyes off of your cash flow. When the money runs out, you're out of business and you should have made a decision to change course well before that ever happens. Never risk the family home and all your retirement savings on what you think is the next billion dollar idea.

Get outside advice if you're struggling. It's a sign of strength to ask for help when you need it. There are many people out there who would be delighted to offer their wisdom and help you out. There are mentorship and mastermind programs to help new start-up businesses. I consider myself extremely lucky to have studied and worked in business.

If you're planning to take your business into uncharted territory, here is what you need to know and do:

1. Write up a short description of your hot new idea and come up with your tag line. Make sure you include your tightly focused target market. **"ALL women will love this"** is not a market, it's half the planet. A clearly defined market is someone you can assign an avatar or representative photo of your ideal client, with age range and detailed personal preferences, their demographics. If you cannot imagine your ideal client, then you're not ready to talk to the money people yet.

2. Once you have your company overview detailing what you want to do and for whom, pick five to ten marketing and sales people you know and talk to them about your ideas. They're the ones who are on the front line selling every day and without sales there is no business! A good sales professional will instinctively recognize a sellable idea.

   See if they agree with your notion of the target client and your messaging. Listen carefully to what they say and make notes because you're bound to get a certain amount of conflicting advice. If you talk to ten people and nine out of ten say your idea is great, then go further. If only a couple say it sounds like a good idea, ask them what would make it better. After your meetings, re-evaluate if you have a viable business or not. Revise your marketing literature with the suggested changes.

3. Next, pick ten to twenty people **in your target market** that can talk to you about your business idea. Explain your idea to them and ask them what they think. Would they buy it and at what price? Test drive different pricing platforms, a low/medium and a high-priced suggestion to see what you can afford to charge. See where the resistance to price comes in. Design a standard list of questions to ask each potential prospect. You can use social media to find these people and even start building your new client base.

   Note: While asking friends and family is great, they want to support you, so their opinions are biased. Don't take what they say as gospel, especially if it conflicts with what unrelated people have told you.

4. If enough of your target clients indicate that they would be willing to buy your product or service then you're ready to get started on a business and marketing plan. People are nice and don't like to say no, that's why you cannot count on 100% of what they say until the money is in your hands.

The Pioneer Patti photo at the beginning of this chapter is of me when I was living on the farm that was almost off the electricity grid. That meant living like a pioneer; hauling wood and water. Our house was built in 1832 and that dress is what a woman of that era would have worn.

THE GARDEN PARTY

....

WHY INNOVATION IN BUSINESS IS
IMPORTANT

After starting Down to Earth Gardens it took a couple of years for me to feel confident in my horticultural knowledge (one eight-week evening course on perennial flowers can only go so far). I had started out in that course knowing only two kinds of flowers—daisies and marigolds.

I knew one was a perennial and one was an annual and I wasn't really sure which was which and why. I was sure that the annual should have been called a perennial and vice versa. I spent the first two years in my new business immersing myself in flowers, trees, and shrubs and reading solely from my ten-foot-high stack of gardening books and magazines.

Into my third season, I was feeling a surge of confidence in my garden knowledge. The farm and my display gardens were finally looking like a real garden centre and I was finally ready for the official opening of my business. However, by the time I came to that realization, I was crazy busy getting ready for my May seasonal opening. I was working ten to twelve hour days, seven days a week. In running a garden centre, you go to sleep in March and wake up in July. It really is a blur.

As I didn't have time to plan for a major "official" opening in early May, I decided I would do an event during the August long weekend. It would be a customer appreciation event since I now had repeat clients to appreciate and celebrate.

I decided to call it the "Garden Party: A Celebration of Summer!" Time to put your hoes down, dress up, and enjoy the garden instead of working on it.

The Sunday of the long weekend in Ontario, either you're at a cottage or you're wishing you were at one and are looking for something to do, especially if it involves getting out of the hot city. So, I invited people to come out for a lovely summer afternoon in the country. They could pet some friendly llamas and lambs, dogs and ducks, have a picnic by the pond, go for a walk in the forest, see some display gardens (that they didn't have to weed), nibble on edible flower cookies and be inspired by new garden-related products.

I solicited other vendors whose products were flower-related, such as herbs, aromatherapy products, garden art, and edible flower creations to attend as well. I threw in a charitable aspect with 10% of sales and donations going to the local animal shelter and we finally had some synergy going. When the local TV station phoned to say that they were coming, I knew I was on to something good.

The first year that I held the party, we had 250 people show up for the two-hour event, with a TV interview and front-page local press coverage. It eventually became the must-attend summer event for gardeners in my area for the next four years. The local press loved it.

Each year it got bigger and bigger until I had to employ a staff of twelve to assist me and had 500 guests in a three-hour crunch. My garden centre became a destination of choice for gardeners who wanted unique, well-priced, "unkillable" plants from an unusual character like myself.

While I never advertised it as a "sale", it was the official start date of my annual summer sale. If I had just put on a regular sale, I would have had to spend a lot of money on advertising. In retail, you have to stand out and do something different in order to be noticed.

The editor of our local paper gave me the tip to have a charitable aspect added to my events. Having a sale is not news, but once you add a charitable aspect, it is. You have to give reporters something newsworthy to report on and then you'll get the publicity that you want.

"Make me care" is what every news release must do to get an editor's attention.

As my garden party was a fundraiser with lots of free activities and displays, I got an incredible amount of FREE publicity both before and after the event. It put Down to Earth Gardens on the map, and our little dirt road would have dozens of cars lined up to get in. A police officer friend helped manage the traffic chaos and parking and we used our golf carts to ferry people and their plants to their cars. It was a fun and relaxing Sunday in the country.

Another reason to not have a typical customer appreciation event is that everyone has them. What is going to make your event different? Use your creative mind and not your chequebook to make your event stand out. You'll most likely end up saving money too in the long run.

Come up with a unique event that is FUN and people might even pay to come to it. In addition, you'll enjoy planning a fun event. Pick the brains of your family, friends, and customers to come up with something special and keep asking what else could make it even better.

Bubbly enthusiasm is contagious. Even though starting a garden centre was never in my wildest dreams, I did thoroughly relish the experience and loved my thousands of "babies", the seedlings which I grew and nurtured into mature plants.

People thought I was living the dream, which could not have been further from the truth. However, I did appreciate most parts of being a farmer, especially when groups of people were around to enjoy our farm.

Running the garden centre made me appreciate how hard farmers worked and how good it felt to be in great physical shape for the first time of my life. Starting and running a successful business from scratch, all by myself, in an industry where I had no background, gave me the confidence that I could truly do anything that I wanted to, but only because I knew how to sell and market. That is key for any and every business.

While I loved aspects of being a farmer, the 24/7 care and feeding of the business (literally, you cannot ignore watering plants for a day) was taxing. I didn't realize how strenuous it was to run a farm-based business. I was never off duty unless I refused to answer the door. To get time off, I'd put up a sign that said, "Sorry I can't be here. If you want to buy a plant, please leave the money in the shed and don't pay any taxes as that's my gift to you for not being there." Early in my farming life, one of my suppliers told me that you can trust gardeners, that they're honest people, and he was right. I'm sure there were a few plant thieves who came and took what they wanted when I wasn't around but I figured in that case they must have needed the plants more than I did.

If I had stopped and taken time off to plan my life between running a tech company and the farm-based business, I probably wouldn't have started the garden centre and that would have been unfortunate.

My life has been amazingly enriched because of living so immersed in nature for those eight years. So sometimes it pays to go with your gut and be spontaneous. Otherwise, you'll talk yourself out of something that could end up being a life-changing experience.

Don't overthink things, sometimes you have to take that leap of faith and just go for it!

So what makes you and your business unique? You might hear it called your USP or Unique Sales Proposition. You need to know and be able to concisely say what makes you different from others in your industry. People who do not know you need to put you in some sort of category. That's how we deal with new people, you get labeled. So be in control and define your own label, make it short and snappy and memorable.

For example, my current business is called the Small Biz Sales Coach–I help you sell more "stuff". I also tell people that I'm really a business growth expert. I look at where you want to grow your business and how sales and marketing and a decent plan and strategy will get you there.

What makes me unique is why you're reading this book. A client asked me recently what job I haven't done. I responded with, "prostitution" as between my clients and me, I've sold and marketed just about everything under the sun.

What FUN, innovative events can you do to make your business stand out and get noticed?

Emphasis is on the FUN. During my barcode days, we had a Barcode BBQ Bash. Alliteration is great for making things easy to remember and flow off the tongue. Why not make it enjoyable?

The cardinal sin in selling and in business is to be boring. So be unique, be memorable, and be profitable. Make any event entertaining and get people talking about you. In this busy world that we live in, we all need to relax, kick back and enjoy life more. And fun makes an event easy to sell.

What kind of party can you put on, and for which charity?

Pick a charity that you truly believe in, one that is close to your heart. As we had adopted a dog and two cats from the local animal shelter, an animal cause was appropriate and something that I've supported personally for years. The bonus is the charity will also publicize your event to their group of followers, which expands your reach.

The press will pick up that it's a community fundraiser and see that it deserves a mention if not front pages photos. Those small community papers pack a punch. Don't ignore them in lieu of trying to get attention with the national papers. Start small and the nationals will eventually come to you.

People buy your enthusiasm for what you do. If you're not enthusiastic about what you do, why should they care? Remember that you need to be your own best cheerleader. If you're not out promoting yourself and your business, then who is?

Do not be a wallflower and stand in the shadows. Be proud of what you do and have done for others and let your prospects know. Helping people be clear and confident in their value is what I do for most of my business clients now as many struggle to articulate what their value is.

Have a brag sheet of what your clients have achieved with your help. Take a look at mine on my website as an example. I always say, "don't listen to me as I'm a sales person. See what my clients have achieved and what they have to say". Unlike mutual funds, my past performances are a great indicator of my positive future results for you.

How can you take your enthusiasm and innovate a new product or service?

Being the cheapest in your category is not fun. You are just a commodity player, betting on people wanting a bargain. Bargain shoppers are not loyal clients either, as many Groupon clients have learned to their detriment and loss. Yes, there's always a market for being cheaper, but NEVER try and compete with Walmart; that's guaranteed suicide for a small business. You do not have their clout or bank roll to beat them.

I was happy when Walmart was coming to my town as their plants were not as hardy and advice was hard to find. Mine were unkillable and priced just a bit more. With me you got sage advice, could see the plant being grown successfully and know that if you had any issues, you knew where to find me and that I'd be delighted to help.

How can you do things differently from your competitors?

When we started the barcode business, a well-established twelve-person subsidiary of a billion dollar company monopolized our city. They abused their position as a monopoly and were a grim group of people to boot. Then we came in, the guerrilla warriors bent on changing the barcode landscape.

We were brash and bold. We knew barcodes. We dressed up at Halloween, we held fun parties and laughed a lot with our clients and prospects. We were open, honest and didn't try to scam clients. We were The Barcode Experts.

We hired the last three employees of the former monopoly as they closed down their business a few years later. Being honest, operating with integrity and being fun to deal with always wins and is what leads to a sustainable business. SageData is now in its 26th year of operation. Congrats to them.

What makes you more fun to deal with than others?
What can you do to surprise and delight your clients?
What joy do you bring to your clients?

BE LIKE A FARMER

....

HOW TO POSITION YOURSELF AS AN EXPERT

People believe the editorial content they see on TV, hear on the radio and read in the paper. They do not totally believe advertisements, since they know the advertiser has paid to be there.

Editorial content wins over ads by a ten-to-one believability ratio. I made up that statistic but I think you get my point; it's big. FREE editorial content is worth a huge amount of money, that's why you see so many product placements in movies and on TV.

The easiest way to get free publicity is to get interviewed. And why would they want to interview you? Because you're the expert, the go-to person, *the* person in your field. You've picked your niche and you've become known for it. Your name has become synonymous with your field of expertise. For example, if you're a marketing expert and a question on marketing arises, then you're the one that reporters will automatically want to go to for an expert opinion.

I don't know about you, but don't you get sick of seeing the same old university professors or consultants being used over and over again for opinions in the media? I do, and I learned from some of them. I'm sure that journalists are just as tired of using them as we are of reading about them. Reporters are always looking for a new, reliable, and quick-responding resource, especially one with contrarian opinions and great quotes.

How do you go about becoming an expert? According to Malcolm Gladwell, it takes about 10,000 hours spent on one subject to qualify as an expert. With a typical 40-hour work week (as if entrepreneurs work that little, ha!), it adds up to about 250 weeks or five years fulltime.

Writing a book, blog or series of articles on your topic is a great way to start establishing yourself as an expert. Speaking in public is another way. Teaching courses will also solidify your expert positioning. I've done all of those in my businesses throughout the years and it really does work.

Another definition of an expert might be anyone who is from 100 miles away or more. Not being local sometimes works to your advantage. The theory is: if you can make it big in your hometown and can afford to start broadening your market, then obviously you know your stuff and have exhausted your local potential. That's how the thinking goes.

With local community papers you can sometimes link a low cost, business card-sized ad with a much longer, more prominent article that positions you as an expert. These articles, even though they're written by a local business with a vested interest, still get noticed, read and believed much more than ads because they appear to be part of the editorial part of the paper.

One Sunday a married couple, Jill and Max, came by my nursery and said they were here because they had seen my article in the local paper. I preened myself, flattered for being recognized as an author and expert. It's so nice to be famous for those five seconds.

So why did they come? I asked. What kind of plants were they interested in? "We're here to buy some of your magnolia trees", they said. That's when I realized that they had read the OTHER nursery's article. I didn't sell magnolia trees—they were too iffy for our local climate. My garden centre was aimed at easy-care low maintenance plants, and magnolias certainly did not qualify.

I hung my head resignedly as I told them, "that's that other nursery…but since you're here, you might as well take a look around. Why do you want a magnolia tree?" (I had a rule about asking probing questions and never turning away a potential customer!)

By taking them on a tour of my gardens and questioning them, I found out that they weren't actually suited to be magnolia tree owners, as the trees need a fair bit of pampering and just the right location; a late frost will take away all of their blooms. Jill and Max were, in fact, ideal owners of my unkillable easy-care plants.

They ended up buying a carload of plants. Not only that, but the next day I got a call from Jill—she loved me and my gardens so much that she wanted to volunteer at Down to Earth! For free! It also demonstrates the power of asking probing questions to discover what people really want or need. I have turned people away without questioning them in the past, and have learned from my mistakes. Sometimes a wrong turn can end up being a right one.

Before I opened the garden centre for my first season, I was asked to do a talk to a small group of beginner gardeners— less than ten people they said. By the time that I did the talk, the group had grown to twenty-five with some experienced gardeners, including the President of my local horticultural society (who knew me as a plant idiot). I was so nervous and scared, but I did it and survived. The only way to get better is to just do it and do the best you can under the circumstances.

With time, I became an accomplished speaker with my own garden groupies and fans. I did know what I was talking about and could tell funny stories about my gardening adventures and those of my clients.

When the late Warren Evans, an old high school friend and long time professional speaker, visited me on the farm and suggested that I could make a six-figure income by simply talking about gardening (never mind actually doing any physical labour) it really made me think about my next career move.

As my hands-on gardening career was coming to a close, I was a featured speaker at the rural industry event of the year— The International Plowing Match. It's a huge six-day event that takes place on over 1,000 acres of farmers' fields. Speaking above the din of the tractors and plows was an accomplishment in the rural world that I was in. It showed that I had earned my stripes both as a horticulturist and as a speaker.

When I started the garden centre, I was just above a beginner level gardener. I had never worked at a garden centre and had no idea what I was doing in that first year. The funny thing is, when you open a business, people just assume you know what you're doing.

Start positioning yourself as an expert as soon as you get beyond the intermediate stage. "Act like the person and business that you want to become, not the one that you currently are", says Terry Matthews, one of Britain's wealthiest men and an Ottawa tech pioneer. Just know when to ask questions to learn more.

Acting like an expert does NOT mean lying if you don't know the answer. Remember, it's easier to keep your stories straight if you stick to the truth. It's the sign of a self-confident person when they can acknowledge what they don't know as easily as sharing what they do. No one has all the answers all of the time.

There is nothing wrong during a sales conversation to admit that you don't know the answer to a question, but that you'll find out and get back to them as soon as possible. Actually following up with the questioner is a trait of a true sales professional and entrepreneur who is really driven to succeed. Under-promising and over-delivering never fails when you're starting a new business, however, doing the reverse is a sure course for failure..

There is nothing like a good sound bite for a quote and call-out to make whatever article you are in even more valuable from a potential sales angle. When you think of the knowledge and wisdom you wish to share, see if you can come up with some pithy quotes that the reporter can use and identify you with. Once you become known for having good sound bites, you'll find that you'll be asked to be back on that TV program or quoted in that newspaper article or asked to speak to a group.

I highly recommend that you watch Gary Vaynerchuk aka Gary Vee's **"One Is Greater Than Zero"** video where he talks about how he hustled for years to get any media attention that he could. He realized the value of reaching out, as you just never know when that one important listener, reader or viewer might be there to give you a ticket to get on the next show or into the next newspaper.

What I love about this video is that it shows how he ended up being an "overnight success" in only ten thousand little steps and a couple of decades. For all those supposed instant overnight successes, the people with the secret sauce and magic formulas who promise to turn you into bajillionaires yesterday, I believe he tells the truth about the other 99.9% of entrepreneurs—the ones for whom "blood, sweat and tears" and sixteen to eighteen hour days are the norm, until they become that success.

The life of an entrepreneur is not easy but it's so worth it! Most entrepreneurs eventually consider themselves unemployable as they couldn't put up with the corporate BS, politics and back stabbing that can go on in some places. So instead they put up with the extreme hours of low or no pay, frustrating staff and lots of expensive life lessons in order to come out with a business that they feel proud to call their own.

What are you an expert in?

What do you want to become an expert in? (As I proved with my garden centre, wanting to be an expert is the first step to becoming one)

What is your driving passion?

What's on your list of things to accomplish before you die or get too old to do?

I BELIEVE IN RIGHTS

....

The **right** product
for the **right** market
with the **right** message
at the **right** time
at the **right** price.

Rights are always important, but especially so in marketing. You have to get a lot of rights lined up in order for your marketing to be effective. You can have the best strategy and plan in the world, but if it's not executed properly and at the right time, it can still fail. If it does fail, it only means that some part of it was off and not necessarily that the whole strategy was wrong.

One of my pet peeves is when I meet with a business owner, who supposedly wants my help, but negates everything I suggest with a "tried it, done it, it didn't work" attitude. Marketing has so many variables that it's impossible to test them all at once. As long as you have a process and tracking mechanism in place, you can figure out what works for you and what doesn't.

That's why testing different subject lines is important to see which one gets more opens and clicks. You can't just assume that one is better than the other until you put it to the test. Testing is everything in marketing success.

Just because you've tried something once, does not mean that it doesn't work. It just means that that combination of your offer and message to that marketplace at that time didn't work. Changing any one of those variables can make a huge difference in your business' future success or failure. You just have to make some adjustments and try again. Repeat until it does work.

Earlier I had mentioned how there's a market for every product. That doesn't mean that every market is right for your product every time. You might have the right product and the right message but the wrong target market. If you don't have the right audience for your message, this illustrates the need for market research and testing.

To find your right market, you need to look at who has bought your product or service in the past and see if there are some common characteristics. Think about how you can group your clients together.

What do your ideal clients have in common?

What interests or geography do they share?

Those are the kinds of questions that you can ask yourself to determine who your ideal client is and what they look like. The more you know about them, the easier it is to write a compelling message to them.

Ask your current clients WHY they bought from you. That will lead you to ask the same questions to prospective clients to see if they could also benefit from your product.

One example of a crucial missing detail that can make or break a marketing campaign was a tag line that I noticed once on the tailgate of a truck in front of me. The slogan was: "**We play** games **with our customers!**" I loved it!

It was a great line, but what company was it from? I'm always on the lookout for great marketing, so I really wanted to know who was responsible for it. I was frustrated by the fact that I could not see who the company was, there was no company name, phone number or website.

A great eye-catching message totally failed to connect me to a company. Talk about a big marketing FAIL (and the fact that the driver gave me the finger as I passed, didn't really add to their fun reputation either).

It's a prime example of how you can do so much right, come up with a catchy slogan that hooks your products with the feeling of what you do for your customers and then totally fail to link it with your company. It doesn't take a rocket scientist to point out the missing link now that you know what to look for.

How many companies fail because they don't think through the smallest of details that are essential to the success of a marketing activity?

Have you had outsiders look at your marketing to see what your blind spot is?

That's why it's called a blind spot—you can't see it. That's why you need a partner, spouse or customer panel/focus group to point out what may be obvious to everyone but you.

Most business owners probably have some education in their field of expertise but have maybe only completed a day course on marketing. However, all of a sudden, they think they know how to market, when in reality they're only just beginning to understand. There is a low barrier to entry for sales and marketing as compared to engineering, medicine or the trades.

The stereotypical salesperson usually talks too much and listens too little to be as effective. The optimistic introvert or ambivert actually makes a better sales person, once they've had some training or coaching in the sales process.

At SageData, the barcode software company, we once hired one of Canada's top direct marketing experts to write a direct marketing letter for us. At the same time, my partner (the engineer and President of the company) and I both wrote our own versions of a direct mail letter. We then bought a list of 3,000 names of our target market and mailed off 1,000 with each letter.

Guess whose letter pulled in the most responses? It was a tie between the President and myself (okay, maybe the engineer's letter pulled in a few more responses, but I called it a tie. It's my book, my story and I get to tell it like I saw it. I hate losing!). The supposed "expert" came in dead last by a significant amount.

What that meant is that after five years of selling barcode systems, both my partner and I knew and understood our target market much better than an outsider. It really depends on your target audience and their profile. Our typical clients were analytical and detail-oriented, which is why my partner's letter worked better than the standard marketing pitch.

However, they also responded to my less flashy benefits-oriented pitch, so they were not completely immune to being marketed to. But it was clear that the typical over-the-top, obvious pitch did not motivate them to action.

"You can be right or you can be in a relationship," said one marriage counsellor and that includes customer relationships too. Is the customer always right? Yes and no. It depends. They are almost always right except when they are being unreasonable. Then no, you have to set boundaries.

For an irate client, all you have to do sometimes is ask "What will make this right for you?" and wait for their answer. Sometimes it's something really simple, inexpensive and so doable. If you ask them what they really want and they only sputter and voice angry comments, then they are really taking out their rage on you. This anger has nothing to do with you and unless you're a therapist, you can't help them. This is when the customer is not right and you just need to say sorry, but no.

So, do you have all your rights lined up?

What have you been doing that is beneficial and profitable?

What part of your marketing activity could be tested in order to improve its performance?

What are the right questions to identify what your prospects want or need from you?

HOW AN IMAGINARY DOG MADE MILLIONS

....

WACKY IDEAS THAT WORK!

After selling many expensive custom-designed asset-tracking programs at our barcode company in the mid 90s, I realized that tracking assets did not differ a lot from one organization to another, especially at federal government departments.

I felt that the world needed a standard low-cost off-the-shelf program that worked on these new industrial hand-held computers. It would use barcodes to easily and accurately track assets such as computers, printers, desks, etc. People needed that system now and not in several months.

Given our custom development backlog and that I was on 100% commission, paid only when the company got paid, I wanted a system that could be sold and installed quickly. My personal cash flow was a huge motivator, but servicing our clients was even more important.

The biggest competitor to our electronic systems was pen, paper and clipboards filled with inch-thick computer printouts.

Typically, some poor summer student would be assigned the menial task of taking asset inventory. They'd get the computer printouts describing that this asset with this asset number should be in this room.

This was all well and good IF that was an accurate record but asset records were generally a mess and rarely updated electronically. If an item had been moved from one office to another, it was a nightmare to reconcile.

Government offices are HUGE (think Pentagon) and usually spread over dozens of buildings in the same city and across the country. Reconciling inventory records manually was a laborious task that inevitably did not get done.

What our system did was electronically reconcile the inventory immediately. The asset records were updated instantaneously and then electronically transferred to the organization's main asset inventory database.

Lying in bed one night, reading the classic book *Positioning* by Ries & Trout, I was trying to figure out what to name my new system. I kept repeating to myself, "Barcode asset tracking, barcode asset tracking, barcode asset tracking" trying to come up with a catchy name for our product like Kleenex did for facial tissues.

I looked at my two dogs who were snuggled down at my feet and thought about how our program was a

tracking system, just like how a hound tracks things. Eureka! Basset (our **Ba**rcode **Asset** Tracking system) was born!

Kim, our receptionist, was a talented artist, and came up with the cutest barcode-equipped basset hound you'd ever seen, complete with Sherlock Holmes' trademark deerstalker hat.

Notice the handheld scanner in it's back pocket? The Basset brand was born and became an instant hit. Well, maybe not quite instant but within a year it was selling nicely and is still being sold today, twenty years later.

The next call-in that I got requesting an asset tracking system, I told them about Basset, confidently telling them "that's what you need, our Basset system!" I then wrote up the marketing flyer inventing the Basset system as I typed and faxed it to them as if it were a real product. To our surprise, within a week, we received a faxed purchase order without having spoken again to that prospect! This had never happened before.

My partner was astounded. In our four years in business together, a sale for a $5,000 system had never been this fast and easy. It was like a dream come true after years of hustling our butts off. I finally met the client when I did the installation and training for them.

My beloved Basset system was installed all over North America, and three other continents. Being used in over 25 countries wasn't bad for a small ten-person software company.

We eventually started a Basset user group, headed by a huge fan of ours—an ex-NATO Colonel turned Brigadier General. He helped us sell a Basset system to the NATO forces in Bosnia which lead to the press release of Basset Barcodes Bosnian Battletanks.

Once we had sold enough systems, we were able to hire more staff to train and support our growing clientele. It took four people to do the work I had been doing by myself I hired an exceptional summer student as my marketing assistant, who eventually became my marketing manager once she graduated.

Some of her ideas were brilliant, like the Basset and Whippet brands. We were selling a $5,000 system and giving away a $5 BassetPro-branded stuffed animal with each system—that was during the Beanie Baby craze.

Clients used to fight over the $5 stuffed toy, so we'd give them two. It was such a cheap and easy way to have our systems front and centre and it reinforced our fun brand too. I always say if we could make selling boring barcode systems fun, you could have fun doing anything.

One year we were so busy selling and installing systems that we missed out on organizing our annual Christmas customer appreciation party. I still wanted to have a party, and thought that February in Ottawa was as good a time as any to celebrate. However, I needed a reason for the party and decided that Basset deserved a birthday party—it was turning two!

I have fond memories of our local mayor bringing in a huge

cake as we all sang "Happy Birthday" to an imaginary dog. 100 people showed up for the party and we gave out cute Basset-branded mugs and t-shirts to our guests. We had a limited marketing budget but we made the most of what we had by being creative and not simply throwing money away on expensive print ads.

Don't get me wrong; we wasted a ton of money on ads in our early days until we knew better. It has lead me to advising my small business clients to use their imagination rather than throwing money at their marketing problems to get better and more fun results.

Why is branding so important?

Think of the value of some brands like Coca Cola, Starbucks, McDonald's, Apple, Disney, Ferrari, Uber and eBay. The top brands are worth billions in name recognition. You know what you get when you purchase a Starbucks coffee versus the local diner's coffee. Or generic cola instead of Coke, it never quite tastes the same but does save you a lot of money. Holiday Inn became a popular chain of hotels, because you were never surprised when you went to one.

Luckily I like surprises and hate conformity. It's boring and so predictable, the death of many a new business. As a small business, you cannot afford to be like all the others. You must stand out or you become irrelevant and eventually go out of business.

You must have a brand promise—mine is "I take you from Sales FEAR to Sales FUN. My business card states: "Have fun and make money" that furthers my 'profitable fun' intentions.

The more fun you have, the more money you will make. AND if you're not having fun, then who cares about the money?

It's important to keep in mind that even if you have a great brand image but no sales, you don't have much of a sustainable company. You have to capitalize on that great brand to increase profitable sales. You snooze, you lose. So don't get caught coasting when you need to be out prospecting.

Remember, nothing matters but sales! Techies and engineers are the worst. They'll spend months and years working on a product only to find that no one can afford it or even wants what they've designed. You see them on TV programs like Dragon's Den and Shark Tank.

They've invested tens of thousands of dollars in patents and trademarks for an unmarketable product. I've had too many clients who have invested thousands of dollars into a product that I felt there was no market demand for. There wasn't anything unique enough to make it a winner. It's so sad.

TEST, TEST, TEST before you sink your life savings into something.

Branding with integrity is important as it gives a value to your business. It provides a face for an otherwise anonymous product. It helps you stand out and differentiate yourself from other similar products. It's what gets you fans and word-of-mouth referrals, the best kind to have.

Think of Sir Richard Branson of Virgin. He's the daredevil we all want to be, isn't he? He's jumped out of planes, broken world records for stunts that would turn anyone's hair grey AND he's always having fun. His family is his #1 priority and

I believe he considers his employees to be part of his extended family.

However, there's a huge difference between branding for a large established corporation like IBM or Virgin vs. a small start-up. Yes, you do need your brand promise (what you stand for, what you do and for whom) but don't spend too much time on your "brand".

Go sell your product or service first, and your customers will help you find your brand. In this day of over-sharing via social media, you are no longer solely in control of your brand and image. Your happy and not-so- happy customers will tell the world about their experiences with your company.

Responding with quick action to the unhappy ones is what will make the difference between flourishing and growing or shrinking and dying. No one is perfect and even the best brands screw up sometimes. We are all human after all.

In these days of social media, your customers now determine your brand. It is what THEY say it is. You can try and have a brand promise and live up to it. However, any deviances from what has been promised, will be Tweeted and posted everywhere for everyone to see.

My brand promise, as the Small Biz Sales Coach, is that I take you from Sales FEAR to Sales FUN and I love to see my clients start having fun when they're making sales.

What I learned from developing Basset was that it didn't hurt to have a loveable mascot to make a boring barcode system more human and more fun. How can you make your product more approachable, more fun?

Given that your clients now determine your brand, it is imperative that you monitor all social media for mentions of your company, products and brand. Google Alerts is ideal for that.

Make sure you respond promptly even if it's just a "We're sorry. What can we do to help? What can we do to make it right?" The success of your brand depends on this.

What is your brand promise?

What do your customers say is your brand?

What do you want it to be?

How can you build a boutique image that lets you charge more for your services (I am sure you are worth it! Most entrepreneurs undercharge when starting out).

WE ARE ALL IN SALES

NO SALES MEANS NO BUSINESS

After I completed my first sales training course at IBM, my mother never trusted me again. She found that I was increasingly evasive and answered every question with a question. I learned that we "sell" all the time; we are all in sales!

Every time we try to persuade someone to see our point of view, that is sales in action. It happens in every relationship, not just in business. If you do not believe this, then read best selling author Dan Pink's book, *To Sell is Human*. While I disagree with how he throws all sales people into one big bucket, he does make the point that we're all in sales ALL the time!

Once I mastered the basics of selling, I thought I had found the magical key to success. I was having conversations where I could get people to do what I wanted them to do and get paid a lot at the same time.

Early in my career, I found out that people hated saying no, that they were almost pre-programmed to say yes to whatever you asked them for—you only had to ask. What a revelation! So for a shy introvert, all I had to do was ask and shut up. Being quiet came naturally to me, and that is so important in closing a sale—ask for the order, then shut up.

My initial sales training was at IBM during my six-month basic systems training that all professionals went through. We learned that the best sale is the one you walk away from, as they are the ones that cause you the grey hairs and are more trouble than they're worth.

In my life as a self-employed entrepreneur, that means not dealing with clients that I don't like or want to do business with. The reason I don't deal with those kinds of companies is that they will suck you dry, take all your knowledge for free and not pay you a cent, which is lethal for a small business. One of the perks of being your own boss is that you can pick and choose whom you deal with.

I remember calling on one high tech company in Ottawa, and just behind the receptionist's desk was a sign reading, "We kill every 3rd salesperson and the 2nd one just left..." Oh joy. During our meeting, we could hear the president screaming abuse at some poor schmuck in another room.

Again, not a company I wanted to do business with, but I felt sorry for the employees who were tasked with finding a system to make the boss happy and unfortunately, we were the only game in town.

At IBM, we were taught to never slag the competition as that only made you look small and petty; advice I still follow today. You must know how you're different from your competition but should never put them down or talk badly about them as it reflects worse on you than it does on them. Sometimes silence is golden when it comes to being asked about your competitors.

At IBM, we were forbidden to use any computer jargon or acronyms during our presentations, thereby making it more customer-friendly. We were told to speak the prospect's language so that they'd understand and didn't feel intimidated by words that they didn't know. A big part of IBM's sales training involved role-playing sales calls, which made actual sales calls with real prospects feel much easier.

During our role-plays, one of the instructors would be the prospective customer while three of our peers would observe us on the call. It was always videotaped for later review. I remember my first practice sales call, before they had taught us anything about selling. It was appallingly bad! Every practice sales call would be marked on twenty evaluation points and everyone would discuss it afterwards. No pressure eh? That's why real sales calls with real prospects seemed like such a treat afterwards.

In my first role-play, I had to try and sell some pencils, but found out, to my horror, that my prospect's brother-in-law had stocked his warehouse with millions of pens! The panicked smile on my face grew even broader as I absorbed this information and had no idea what to do next.

During the role-playing, he took my pencil and deliberately broke the tip of it, leading me to introduce the imaginary pencil sharpener, my first ever improv session. What this illustrates is that selling is a skill that can be learned.

I was not a natural born sales person, but I did get points for persistence. Being good in sales takes a lot of face-to-face practice, knowing the techniques and making them your own and developing a proverbial thick skin.

There is no shortcut to having 100 sales conversations to get the 'spiel' right and it has to flow off your tongue naturally. You just have to do them.

As Churchill said, "If you're going through hell, keep going" and the same advice applies to sales training. It's hell until you succeed and as an entrepreneur, you must succeed at selling. Sales conversations get easier the more you do them and the more success you have as you get better at the Sales Game.

Being the only Patti Pokorchak in the world, means that I have my own unique style that clearly works, as demonstrated by my successful sales history. I found I was really good at selling intangibles, the things that you can't put your hands on, like services and training.

This isn't something everyone can do as I found out being a sales manager and mis-hiring other sales professionals. I had a gift for making things come alive with words, examples and testimonials.

The value of a service was taught to me during one sales call where I realized that I was ten times more expensive than the incumbent consultant, yet still won the business. Boy did

I sweat that sales call, having to ask for $10,000 a day when the competition was only $1,000 a day and a consultant that they already knew and loved.

It was when I exposed the *real* cost of a training day being the twenty engineers' time (which was huge compared to the cost of any course alone) that got the sale. Without slagging off their consultant, I just wondered if a one-off course would offer the same benefits as a course that had been given to tens of thousands of engineers around the world by a proven instructor.

Doubt, fear, having a well-established training course and our instructor's great course evaluations helped win their business. I planted a seed of doubt in the client's mind and that is what it took to win their business.

It showed me that price does not always matter, it's value. **People buy value.** And they will always find the money if you show the value to them.

While we live in a world, at least in North America, where our wants dictate our purchases rather than our needs (the old but working TVs being replaced by the new flat screen TVs), people will still shop around for a deal. You hear about items being sold as commodities.

That's where it becomes hard to distinguish one product from another and that's when people buy based on price and possibly customer service, depending on the complexity of the product.

This is the reason Walmart has succeeded as well as it has. It offers much of what the time-constrained individual needs, all in one place—from school supplies to drugs to groceries to clothes, all at decent prices. Okay, so the clothes won't last a lifetime, but at those prices, who cares? They'll be outgrown or out of style before they wear out. In the meantime, they satisfy a need to shop, to get something new and not break the bank. They are the retail therapy experts.

Sales skills and training for an entrepreneur is crucial in order for the new business to survive and thrive. Especially as an entrepreneur, you have to always be selling and promoting your products whenever and wherever you see an opportunity.

That might be at your kid's soccer game, at the supermarket, on the street, walking your dog—wherever and whenever the opportunity presents itself. The entrepreneurial salesperson never stops working until they feel secure with their bank statement.

Once you get established you can hire sales talent, but in the beginning sales and self-promotion are some of the skills that you must master.

If you say you hate sales—learn to change your opinion or find a job, as you won't make it as an entrepreneur. Unless you've got the financing to hire a hotshot sales pioneer right from the start, your fledgling business will be in mortal danger.

Sales is NOT a dirty word; you're simply helping people to buy from you.

We live in a society where the majority of our needs are met and we shop mainly for our wants. If you're a person with strong morals and ethics, then you'll never force someone to buy something that they cannot afford or do not need or want.

People will remember you and come back to you when they know that you've dealt with them honestly. That's when you'll get the referrals and that's when they can trust that you really do have their best interests at heart and are not out to make a quick buck.

Selling can be fun when you approach it with the right attitude. If you haven't had any sales training, I highly recommend it as the fastest way to make your business successful and profitable. I don't believe that there are born salespeople; we all need to be trained. Those so-called born sales people – they need to learn how to shut up and listen in order to sell more.

The best salespeople are actually quieter people than you would imagine them to be. The old saying goes, "you've got two ears and one mouth and should use them in that proportion", that's how a previously shy and quiet person like myself became great at sales.

Be curious and caring and you'll be a great sales person. When I had to dig deep to find out my "secret sauce to sales", I realized it was caring more about the client's needs and wants being satisfied first, not lining my own pocket at any cost to a prospect.

I've never sold anyone something that they did not need nor want. I sleep well at night knowing I've been of service to others.

My favourite, and most difficult sales call, was when I was working with Rene, our "Presentation Consultant". He didn't like to be referred to as a telemarketer but that was what he was. We had a sales system where we'd put on a half-day seminar on "Everything You Wanted to Know About Barcodes but Were Afraid to Ask".

We used to put on the seminar for free but once we started charging for it, we lost all the under-employed consultants looking for free education and donuts and actually made money on the event.

After the seminar, Rene would make the follow-up calls and book appointments for me as these were prime prospects, or you could say that they had been primed for me to close some business.

Unless I had spent time with the prospect at the seminar, I was going in blind, my version of "business improv", which kept me from being bored. I never knew whether to expect one or twenty people at my "presentations", which were really just sales calls.

Rene had booked me for a full day of sales calls in Toronto starting at 9:00 am at a major multimedia organization. I felt very confident since the prospect had sat through our entire seminar, which meant he was already educated on what fabulous things you could do with industrial handheld computers and barcodes.

I walked into his office and saw every certificate of every workshop he had ever been to, including WordPerfect 5.0, WordPerfect 5.1 and WordPerfect 5.2—ancient word processing programs you've probably never heard of. But you get the idea; there was major insecurity here.

He was sitting behind his desk with his arms crossed (closed body language if you've ever seen it), and a grim look on his face when he told me that he had listened to our spiel and didn't need any of it. I wondered why he had agreed to see me if he had already decided that he didn't need any of our products?

What a way to start a week and a long day of sales calls. I had an hour to kill before my next appointment, so decided, what the heck, might as well ask him some questions. I asked and asked and asked and finally found his sore spot—the delivery of courier packages within that huge building was a major problem.

Eureka! He did need something I was selling. Courier numbers were sixteen to twenty digits long, easily scannable in milliseconds with a barcode scanner, as compared to the time consuming and error prone hand written logs. I walked out with a purchase order, something that had never happened in my previous five years of selling these systems.

Getting a purchase order at a sales call just didn't happen, especially after the kind of frosty welcome I had received. By asking the right questions and not giving up easily (yay Persistent Patti!), I found his pain and was able to give him a fast and simple remedy for it.

It showed me that through the use of effective questioning, I could help the client figure out where his pain was and help him to alleviate it even when he didn't know it existed. A sales professional is most effective when they act like consultants, asking the right questions to get to the core of the problem.

It was when I started my garden centre and hobby farm, where I knew nothing about running a rural retail operation, that I understood knowing how to sell and market can make you successful in any business you're passionate about. Sales and marketing is the one thing that ALL businesses have in common and which all entrepreneurs MUST master.

A business only gets started once a sale is made. So go sell something to a stranger and that will show if you'll have a successful business or not. Selling to friends and family do not count as real sales.

No Sales = No Business, plain and simple.

People buy from people they know, like and trust. If they don't like you, they won't buy from you but if they don't trust you, they will *never* buy from you.

DON'T BE BORING

....

STORIES SELL

At my software company we were branded as "The Barcode Experts" but I felt that I was also in the story-telling business, I mean, barcodes simply aren't that compelling unless you tell some interesting stories to get people engaged.

Luckily, I was involved in barcoding all sorts of things like computers and chairs as well as cows, monkey cages, manure spreaders, bus ads, fire hydrants, garbage cans, boxes of meat and highly confidential government documents (which I was not allowed to look at so had to scan with my head turned away). All this, thankfully, made for some pretty entertaining stories.

One of my personal favourites was about the time we were tasked with doing the Privy Council Office's asset inventory; spread over seventeen buildings in downtown Ottawa. Our inventory technician, Greg, was in the Prime Minister's office completing the inventory. In any executive's office, you had to put the barcode where it wasn't easily noticeable, so Greg was underneath the Prime Minister's desk applying the barcode sticker.

One of the Prime Minister's Member of Staff walked into the office at that moment and saw a stranger fiddling around underneath the PM's desk and ordered him to get up with his hands up.

Greg crawled out from under the desk holding his handheld barcode scanner (that looked oddly like a futuristic weapon from Star Trek) and in his inimitable style and Colombian accent said, "Don't worry; it's only set to stun!" Telling this story allowed us to shamelessly boast about our highest profile client while also inciting a laugh or two.

Another time we were asked if we could tattoo a barcode onto a person's arm, which we graciously declined to do. Body art wasn't really our line of business, but again, it was a story that we could tell to our clients and prospects to make them laugh. We loved the challenge of difficult places to put barcodes.

Making people laugh relaxes them and more importantly, helps people to trust you. Entertaining clients with relevant stories to their situation is a way to advance your relationship. Your customers will be more loyal as they will look forward to your visits instead of expecting another boring sales call.

When I had my garden centre business, I used to joke that I was really in the moving business. I calculated that I moved each and every plant and pot between ten and twenty times, and seeing as I grew thousands of plants each year, that meant there was a whole lot of moving going on. Basically my day was one big game of musical plants until they got sold.

All joking aside, I knew that my core business was to sell easy-care flowers to people who didn't know much about plants and didn't want to either. The other goal of my garden centre/ hobby farm was to be an oasis of nature for urban refugees. We had interesting stories to tell about our animals—we had llamas and lambs, dogs and ducks, barn cats, rabbits, an alpaca and the odd goat or two.

Visitors would sometimes get queasy learning where their food really came from. We raised Katahdin sheep, a breed of hair sheep, developed in the United States and named after Mount Katahdin in Maine. When people would ask what we did with these wool-less sheep, as there was no wool to use and sell, I'd reply, "it *is* a farm after all…" and watch as it slowly dawned on them that that's where their lamb chops came from.

Our lambs had the same names each year—Yummy and Tasty, Roast and Chops—and oh, how they lived up to their names. My first job at sixteen was being a meat wrapper in a supermarket. Who knew those skills would ever be of use to me again as we weighed, packaged and sold our lambs.

Telling stories in business makes your product or service come alive. It gives the intangible some substance and life. The hero of your story must always be a happy customer. Most of my clients did not consider me to be a "salesperson" but just "that nice lady Patti" who came in and chatted to them and told them some funny but relevant stories (while also leaving with a hefty purchase order). I'd relay another client's successes to them and illustrate the highs and lows of that particular installation.

There is a difference between a sales pitch and telling entertaining stories. When you use actual examples of problems and challenges that are similar to what your prospect is trying to overcome, you engage with the individual. It shows your expertise in a way that is not showing off since it's a fact. It's a way of bringing a testimonial to life.

I tell my coaching clients **do not bore people.** That is THE cardinal sin when promoting your business.

Do you want to deal with a boring person? If you had a choice, wouldn't you choose to speak with someone who is fun and approachable?

When I was a headhunter (executive search partner), one of our criteria in choosing which candidates to present to our client was: would you want to spend five hours traveling in a car with this person? In business, there's often a lot of travel involved, which means sitting or standing around waiting. Having a fellow traveller with a friendly demeanor and stories to share makes the trip less tedious.

Boring is bad no matter what situation, and you do not have to be a stand-up comic in order to promote effectively. You only have to know what questions to ask and then actively listen, saying as little as possible as you only learn when listening not talking. That makes you fascinating. Yes, not talking makes you more interesting.

We all have stories. If you don't feel like you're a good storyteller, then all you need to do is practice with someone willing to listen to you (there are story coaches out there) and ask how you can improve, much like getting presentation training. Getting to the point of the story quickly is key. Being too long-winded leads to more sales loss than you can imagine. Bored people tune out and you'll end up losing the sale.

Here are the most important things to keep in mind when using stories in sales:

- Keep the build-up short, say only what is relevant to that prospect
- Explain the problem you solved
- Make your client the hero
- Explain how your solution resulted in amazing ROI (return on investment)
- Ask how you can help them
- Ask for the order!
- If they say "no", ask why not?

If you can make your story entertaining and possibly self-deprecating, that's great! The more interesting your story is, the better. Practice makes perfect, like anything else. The more often you tell your core stories, the better they get as you can tell at what point people tune out and when they engage.

With your own business, you'll generally be advised to come up with a mission statement, value proposition and all that MBA business stuff. However, I'd like you to think about what other businesses you're in.

How else do you connect with your clients in a way that makes you memorable?

What stories can you tell about your product or service and how they're being used to get people to connect to it emotionally?

Once you get their emotions involved, getting them laughing and feeling, then you've got them captivated. People buy with their hearts (despite what you logical types might think).

Donald Cooper, MBA, a great tell-it-like-it-is business speaker and coach, says, "Whatever business we're in, people come to us for that, **plus joy**. They want a new car, plus joy; groceries, plus joy; mutual funds, plus joy; a new computer, plus joy".

So, what are your compelling stories?

Are you telling them well?

How are you bringing joy to your clients?

What value do you offer and how can you make that into a client success story?

Have you written up these success stories and posted on LinkedIn, Twitter, Facebook or your blog?

All businesses have compelling stories or they're not in business for long. Make sure yours are as entertaining and relevant as possible. Practice and get feedback. Then watch your sales soar!

WHERE DID YOU GET YOUR T-SHIRT?

....

THE POWER OF QUESTIONS TO CHANGE YOUR DESTINY

I t was my second month in Munich and I was living in a trendy part of town, enjoying the sights—and of course the beer. My favourite beer garden was the Chinese Tower, located in the English Gardens.

It made for a nice destination after a leisurely bike ride (but who really needs an excuse to drink beer in Munich). It is SO delicious and tasty on a hot summer day, beer isn't even considered alcohol in Bavaria.

So there I was sitting in the beer garden one afternoon when I noticed that the guy clearing the empty beer steins from the tables was wearing a University of Toronto t-shirt. I was somewhat homesick for Canada at the time, as I had been away for almost six months, and I innocently asked him, **"Where did you get your t-shirt?"**

After a short conversation, where I happened to mention that I had once worked as a waitress, I was taken to his boss and briefly interviewed for a job. My lack of fluency in the German language was overlooked because they desperately needed an experienced server to handle the summer rush.

Little did I know I would get my most important German language lessons on the job, for instance, Schweinsekrustenbraten means crispy roast pork!

The next day (and for the next two weeks) I found myself wrapped up in the traditional German dirndl, or folk costume, waitressing huge platters of Schweinsekrustenbraten and lots more Schweine-related items in Munich's busiest pedestrian area. None of this would have occurred if I hadn't asked an innocent question about a t-shirt.

I learned more German in those two weeks waitressing than I had in the previous six weeks of living in Munich. I also learned about the kindness of strangers, like the day I had to look after the pedestrian area patio of 100 seats by myself, which was normally a two-person job.

Two of my regulars could see I was run off my feet and told me to just focus on putting the beer orders in and they'd make sure they all got delivered. I rewarded them later with free beer.

I once asked someone I was coaching, **"What do you regret not doing in your life?"** The client was a talented comedian/

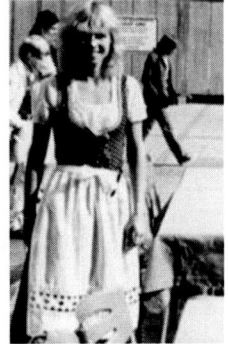

actress/writer who had put on seven one-woman shows and been on major television stations.

Years ago she had been about to move to L.A., when she met the future father of her children, someone who she thought was her soul mate. She interrupted her promising career to marry her husband and become a mother.

My asking her that one question motivated her to go back to L.A., restart her acting career and add a new one-woman show to her repertoire. Unfortunately her marriage did not survive this change but it shows the power of a question to make people sit-up and take inventory of their life and where they are. That is what makes good coaching so life-changing.

Last summer I had to get my passport renewed. It was the typical everyone-is-going-away-on-holidays-soon crowded waiting room. I had at least an hour to kill, waiting to submit paperwork.

Surveying the busy room, I steered away from the crying babies and being single, thought—why not pick a cute guy to sit next to? You never know (that's the optimist in me). I found one and sat down with a smile (it doesn't cost anything to smile does it?)

It felt natural to strike-up a conversation, leading with **"where are you headed to?"** It was the Passport Office after all and travel would obviously be a common interest of all there. We discussed travel plans until we inevitably spoke about what we do for work.

He told me he was a sales director about to launch a small business sales program. I excitedly pointed out to him that my company name is Small Biz Sales Coach. What a perfect fit! I managed to land a contract that I wouldn't have gotten if I hadn't started that conversation.

I've given you three examples of where I used questions: to get a job, land a contract and to change someone's life—all of those things because I broke that ultimate mother's rule to not talk to strangers.

That one question in Munich started a life-long curiosity about people. I'm always talking to strangers and asking them questions. It makes life so much more interesting to interact with people you meet in your daily life.

Many people go through life without any interaction with the hundreds of people they see daily. I notice it most when I take a commuter train downtown during rush hour. People are busy looking at screens or reading, few look excited about their day or bother to talk to one another. It makes me sad.

Having a dog, I'm outside at least twice a day, walking her and making new friends. You can find out someone's story in a few minutes at a park or at a bus stop if you only take the time to ask. It takes a bit of curiosity and lots of caring to get to know someone and it also helps to make their day a bit brighter.

Being curious and caring is my secret sauce to why I have sold so much in my life. I'm authentically curious about people and what makes them tick and I want to get to know them better. People love to talk about themselves; it relaxes them and opens them up for a deeper conversation about their needs, wants and goals, which is exactly the atmosphere that can contribute to a sale!

What questions could you ask in the future that could take you on a surprising adventure?

What chance encounter with a stranger might take your business to the next level or teach you a valuable life lesson?

What opportunities are you missing out on by not asking questions?

When you're out networking are you prepped with questions to ask people that are different from the expected "so what do you do?"?

Alternate questions could be asking them what made them come to this particular group or event, how they found out about it, who they've met that's interesting and what they hope to get out of the event. And, most importantly, **how can you help them?**

Who can I connect you with?

We've all probably experienced the "show up and throw up" style of pitching. You know the one person who always comes into a group and starts dealing out their business cards as if they were at the casino.

When people ask me how to close more business, I say, **"Ask better questions!"**

Questions are the key to success as an entrepreneur. Listening, not talking, is how you close more sales. Get the prospect talking about themselves and their business and they will reveal what their challenges are and what their targets are. That is pure gold.

It's then up to you to show that you can help them achieve those goals. If you can do ten things but they are only interested in one or two, don't bore them with the other eight. They don't care and you might end up talking yourself out of a sure sale. No one likes monologues, especially when you're pitching.

Even if a prospect says, "come and pitch me", do not pitch until you have asked qualifying questions to see what specifically they want from you. Identify their pain points first, then solve only that pain and NOT every conceivable pain that they might have.

We all can do so much but each client usually only needs a small part of our talents to start with. So do not bore them with a laundry list when they only want their ties cleaned.

Make a list of what questions move your prospects towards how you can help them. What questions will qualify them to work with you? What questions determine if they are a qualified prospect, for instance, are their sales stalled? Have they ever had any sales training?

Do they know about the sales process and discipline to close more business? Those are some of the questions I ask as a sales coach to see if someone has the pain that I can solve! To me, a sales conversation is a gently and naturally guided one that leads you both to a place where you get an order.

Ask better questions – close more business. Ask more questions, have a more interesting life. You only learn when listening, not speaking. So stop pitching, and start asking and listening.

ANALYSIS PARALYSIS

How to Plan and Pivot

I will never go to university

I will never become a farmer.

I will never move back to Toronto.

I will never get married.

I will never say never again.

None of the above is true. I did go to two universities, became a farmer, got married and moved back to my hometown of Toronto after years away.

Who knew that all this would happen, even if it was never in my plans?

I call it that the **dreaded "P" word: PLAN.** My dear sister says every family needs a planner, and it's just not me. Yes, plans are needed but don't spend too much time planning and not doing. The only way to see if you're on the right path is to move forward.

Stop preparing to get started and just start. It's that simple. Hold your nose and dive in. It's the ONLY way to see if what you're pursuing is valid or not.

Having started six businesses in the first five years I was back in Toronto, I know what it's like to think something is a good idea, try it, then go, "Geeze, that wasn't what I thought would happen!" Many times I've sat and brainstormed a list of what I want in my life.

The only way to get what you want is first *to know* what you want. Writing things down helps define what you want or don't want. Sometimes knowing what you do NOT want is easier to define, and then what you want might be the opposite of what you don't want.

It sounds more complicated than it is. For instance, if you hate working at a large corporation, then what you really want might be the opposite—working for a small business or even starting your own business.

Should you be stuck doing something just because it was in "the plan"? Absolutely not! It's dangerous for so many reasons. Just because something seemed like a good idea at the time, when you're an entrepreneur just starting out or in times of turmoil and uncertainty, it can be fatal to be so inflexible.

Plus, things can change in the economy and with your target market in an instant.

As an employee, what might have seemed like your dream job can turn out to be a nightmare (like my last corporate job where I lasted seven horrendous months, waiting to get paid what I was owed before resigning). Don't stay stuck—you're not a tree, you can and should move.

Plans change as change is a constant of life and you need to adapt to circumstances. Since when has anything in life ever worked out completely according to plan? Only in your dreams.

The last few two times I came up with some longer-term plans, real life had plans of its own. I bought my second flat in London thinking I was pretty settled and that I'd be there for another two or three years. However, within six months, I unexpectedly moved back to Canada after a nine-year absence.

That was definitely not in the plan, but I was offered a great job that involved the company paying for my move back home and it just felt like the right thing to do.

My second house in Ottawa was a five-year fixer-upper project. I had just come out of a ten-year relationship with my business and personal partner and was happy to have my own place to focus on. I took a year to grieve the relationship and then decided I was ready to start casually dating, emphasis on the casual part.

In 1999, online dating had just started being a thing. Being the techie geek that I am, that was the first place that I was going to try. It took some weeding out and one horrible date before I met Pierre.

Marriage had never been in my plans but eventually I found myself saying "yes" to his "will you marry me?" I moved in with him on his farm exactly a year after I had bought that house in Ottawa. Remember that five-year fixer-upper I was excited to work on? Gone. So much for plans when life and love got in the way.

That was when I started saying; "never say never" as the next big change in plans came along. It happened as a result of being burnt out from running that software company.

The challenge and thrill of it was gone after ten years. I had always said I'd never work in retail or in the gardening business, yet that's when I found myself opening Down to Earth Gardens.

This just goes to show you that plans can be good, but they can also stunt growth. Sometimes you can overthink things and that stops you from doing what you should be doing.

Sticking to plan can make you risk-adverse when the beauty of life sometimes lies in living on the edge and doing things that cause you a bit of fear.

When you update and expand your plans on a regular basis, only then do you grow and change, learn and adapt and become a more diverse person.

Life is uncertain, live with no or few regrets and do what you fear the most as that will make you stronger, more resilient, and more adaptable. That first big change can be scary but it does get a lot easier the more you do it.

It is said that the only certainty is change, so why fear it? Embrace it, search it out, love it, have fun with it and laugh at what life throws at you. It's a whole lot better than burning out, being miserable, avoiding things or taking the safe route. Does playing it safe really add to your life or does it stifle all growth?

As I write this, I'm living in my hometown of Toronto, the place I "never" ever expected or planned to live in again. I call it the thirty-year detour, as that's how long it took me to arrive back from my "one year" of travel. Talk about a plan gone astray!

Not to say that having a plan is always a bad thing, but many people plan too much and do too little. This can be a fatal flaw for an entrepreneur. A good plan executed is ten times better than an excellent plan that is not implemented. It is better to have done something, failed, and learned from your efforts rather than to not have done anything because of inaction.

Don't overthink things. **You can adjust the sails but you've got to get the boat into the water first!**

You will never be able to come up with the perfect plan. Life is just not that predictable, no matter what guru you have on your side. There are just too many variables.

So, do I still make plans? I do. I plan for this week, maybe next week. After that? Who knows! I keep my options open. I have broad life goals so I do know the direction I'm steering toward and what I plan to accomplish this year, but beyond that—well, let's just say I like to be surprised!

What about your plans?

How far ahead do you plan?

Do you know what you want in life?

What do you have to do to achieve those goals?

How do you adjust your plans when life interferes?

GOOD ENOUGH IS ENOUGH!

....

JUST GET IT DONE!

I t's become obvious to me after years of dealing with academics and corporate bureaucrats that entrepreneurs and small business owners need a different mindset when it comes to getting things done. They need a mindset that says, "good enough is enough"—not perfect, but enough to get whatever you're working on out the door.

Annette Verschuren, past President of Home Depot Canada, was recently profiled in Canadian Business magazine with the title "Mediocre Strategy, Brilliant Execution", and that's something I can relate to.

I am a doer! I get things done. Compare me to the Energizer Bunny; I keep on going and going and going—as a busy entrepreneur, that's not a bad way to be.

Don't spend too much time planning and strategizing to the detriment of actual doing, as plans never work out the way you think they will. There are lots of zigs, zags and pivots when it comes to running your own business, especially in that crucial first couple of years.

Despite having started ten businesses in my lifetime, my first year as the Small Biz Sales Coach was full of missteps, mistakes, and many lessons.

Dotting every "i" and crossing every "t" is less important than actually completing a task—something is almost always better than nothing. Perfection has its price, and especially in small organizations it can be way too high, and can result in missed opportunities, lost money, or even going out of business.

Good enough does not mean you're being lazy or taking shortcuts, you do the best you can with the resources and time available to you. It's like the opportunity/cost calculation that an accountant makes, you determine how to best invest your money in order to earn more in the long run.

Good enough is asking yourself a strategic question: with my limited time and resources, **what is the ONE thing that will get me the most traction in my business right now?**

"Only 20% of your time should be spent planning."
Annette Verschuren, past President of Home Depot

Where will I get the biggest payback in terms of my time and money?

You need to ensure you're making the most efficient use of your time. Could you be doing two or even three things to further your business instead of dwelling on the perfection of executing one task?

In a small business, doing two or three things fairly well is much better than doing one thing perfectly. The victim of perfectionism is usually the sustained viability of an organization. When we "over-plan", we hit a point of diminishing returns.

For instance, I know that in order to give an effective talk I need an engaging and professional Powerpoint presentation. A good presentation might take me two days to produce, which is a good use of my time as I'm assuming I will get some sales leads from the event and perhaps a contract.

However, if I spend an additional two hours finding perfect photos for each slide, the extra two hours I spent "perfecting" it will not really bring much more value. I will have hit the point of diminishing returns and I will have been better off doing a new task instead of overdoing something that was already good enough.

When you work for a large organization, you might have the resources, time and budget to achieve perfection (or as close as you can get with time and budget constraints). You might have staff that you can delegate parts of a project to. You may be able to hire a consultant, complete studies and research or hold customer forums—all those time-consuming activities that would be nice, but for small start-ups are quite unrealistic.

What has kept me safe in life are my gut instincts. I somehow know when to walk away from a situation that makes me feel uncomfortable, and I've certainly put myself in places that were not comfortable.

In business I've used those same gut feelings to tell me if a prospect is worth pursuing or not. For example, I learned to sense when someone telling me "not yet" meant "not ever". It was the shifty eyes, the insincere smiles, and the smallest little details in their body language that were unspoken but spoke volumes.

At the same time, that gut instinct (based on thousands of sales calls) also alerted me to a hot prospect—get that proposal to them NOW and close that sale.

I remember once aggressively bumping my partner off of his own computer in order to write up a quote for an order that would close that day. I just knew it would. Speed is of the essence when someone is in buying mode.

Even though we didn't have a lot of competition in the barcode business, I never wanted to waste a second if I sensed that an order was imminent. Did I mention that I was only paid upon the sale happening? That was huge motivation for me to get that deal closed.

Most anything you do can be improved upon and some people continuously delay pressing the send key or completing a project, as they feel that it's never quite good enough. That kind of perfectionist thinking and non-action can be fatal for an entrepreneur. "Good enough" means getting things done ASAP—not later, when opportunities can be missed. Remember that if you snooze, you lose.

All this being said, no one is perfect. I can be accused of not planning enough. However, this isn't always a bad thing. If I had taken some time off between my high-tech life and starting my farm to think about what to do next, I probably would not have become a farmer and my life wouldn't have been as rich and full of adventure.

When I was with my last employer, I had two job offers. I sat with a friend and went over the pros and cons of each offer as they were with two differently sized organizations. I chose the larger of the two and what a disaster that was, the most miserable five months of my life.

Never again will I do something just for the money. So as you see, there can be consequences of being too full of logical plans, there is always room for spontaneity in life.

The fact that I don't write five-year strategic plans and create spreadsheets does not mean that I do not strategize. In fact, after years of experience, successes and misses, I am able to quickly process and assess in my head and make strategic choices.

For example, I was involved in a bid at a major telecommunication organization to give their engineers project management training. This organization was being faced with the prospect of deregulation and competition. I had to work with Peter, an independent entrepreneur and very stressed out project management instructor, to help close the deal.

Before one sales call, he asked me for my project plan on how I intended on winning this business. It was an appropriate question, coming from a project manager, but he forgot who he was dealing with—a sales manager. Us sales pros are not big on detailed plans; we'd rather be out selling something.

My plan lived in my head and gut, not on paper like most of the people that he was used to working with. Peter reamed me out royally for being "unprepared", but I knew that I was doing the right thing, with the right people and at the right time.

I had had several years of experience in negotiating large training projects and was able to see in my head all the steps that needed to be completed in order to close a sale. It was going to take time, especially because engineers have their own plan and process to navigate.

We did win the million-dollar contract, in spite of me not having a written plan. My client also referred to me as the most laid-back sales professional he had ever dealt with. That was just my style and it still is. It's what I train my shyer clients to do, do not act like that pushy aggressive sales jerk that we all hate, but act like yourself. How hard is that? Be curious and caring, ask better questions and you will close more business.

So what does "good enough" look like to an entrepreneur? It looks like a multipage website with sample menu, photos, and all background information instead of a holding page that says, "Coming soon…"

Having a website with all the bells and whistles six months from now will never be as beneficial to you as a good enough website right now. Cash will never flow if you're not out promoting yourself and your products as much as you can as soon as you can.

Good enough looks like sending out an e-newsletter to only 100 people, instead of waiting to grow your mailing list.

Once you get a small portion of those 100 people buying from you, they'll bring in friends and referrals that become your new customers and just like that your mailing list grows to a 1,000+ names.

Remember: **you get to a million customers one customer at a time.** There is always that first customer, the tenth, then the hundredth and so on.

Good enough also means writing a newsletter or blog post of one pertinent, well thought out, informative paragraph and a call to action (always ask them to do something), rather than waiting for those amazing words of wisdom that never seem to make it out of your head and into your target market's sphere.

A regular short nugget of vital information is much more effective, especially when compared to sending nothing out.

Liken it to this old Chinese saying:

When is the best time to plant a tree? Twenty years ago.

When is the second best time? Now.

Same thing goes for business, now is the time to do something to further your business. So rather than waiting longer and delaying doing those things that are important for your business, do what's feasible for you now.

For example, you can set yourself an achievable goal such as making at least ten prospective calls, ten follow-up calls and writing ten emails to prospects every day.

Plan your next event and know how you're going to publicize it and get people to attend. Make every day an improvement over the previous day. That's how a successful business grows.

Warren Evans, the late noted trends blending expert and my good friend said, "Success is the disciplined execution of a **good** idea". It is not the endless search for a brilliant new idea that never gets implemented.

Success is all about action, not analysis without any action. Lack of action results in a dead business, plain and simple.

Where in your life have you been holding back, waiting for the perfect moment?

What's preventing you from moving forward?

How can you motivate yourself to get moving?

Where are you good enough to get going?

Just do it!

Ask for forgiveness, not permission is the motto for successful entrepreneurs and has been my lifelong motto since I realized that people did not like saying no to me. What a true gift for me to learn early in my career.

NETWORKING OR NOT WORKING

....

THE POWER OF CONNECTING

New Year's Eve is typically a big night of fun and celebration, highlighted by a kiss from your sweetheart at midnight. I had kissed my future husband on the night of the big millennium celebration of 2000.

Nine years later, he was my ex-husband. I grieved our marriage for the obligatory year but in 2010 I was ready to get back into the dating scene.

I had been invited to a married friend's suburban house for the evening and being freshly single, agreed with my brother that I should probably stay away from bars on the big night. Hours later I found myself searching online for singles parties at bars, found one and then bought myself a ticket. There's more to life than playing it safe!

It does take a certain amount of courage to walk into a singles event on your own, especially if it's on New Year's Eve. However, since starting my solo travels in Europe in 1980, I had gotten accustomed to trying new things alone.

It's only uncomfortable the first few times that you do something on your own, but how else are you going to meet new people? You have to start somewhere and that means doing things on your own. It doesn't take long to start making new connections, but as a newcomer you have to be the one to stretch your neck out first.

Being the pragmatic businesswoman that I am, I went to the New Year's Eve party with three goals in mind: meet three guys, get a kiss at midnight and leave with a guy's phone number. I met all my goals that evening—I got my kiss, a walk to the car and a phone number. Mission accomplished.

But to me, the biggest accomplishment was just going. It was my first time out alone in a long time and I did it! I felt on top of the world and capable of doing anything. It doesn't take much to get your confidence back but you can only get it back by doing something.

I found this first singles event, which I attended in my fifties, to be more like a business networking event. The meat market scene of my twenties and thirties had disappeared, which I found to be both good and bad news.

Who would have thought that you could ever miss being whistled at, ogled or hassled when trying to have a quiet drink? Sigh. I do miss that attention, however annoying it was at that time. It's like being called "Ma'am" instead of "Miss", something my younger feminist self once bristled at. Please call me Miss now, it makes my day.

When going to a networking event, you should always be prepared with goals. If you can get the attendee list in advance, you can target certain people that would be beneficial for you to meet. It's important to acknowledge why you are going to this event and not simply because you know you need to network. Make effective use of your time by doing some homework. Think about what you have to offer and what you are expecting from those you will meet.

I like to make use of my time in the car, driving to the event, to practice my description of who I am and what I do. I like to try out new introductions to keep things fresh. Some people call it an elevator pitch.

Essentially, this is your ten-to-twenty second infomercial where you detail who you are, what you do and why you're the best person for a job. Your pitch should include what you can do and for whom (your target market). Think benefits, not features and try to make it snappy but err on the side of being clear, not clever.

Here are my current answers for when someone asks me what I do:

I help entrepreneurs be clear and confident in their value, so that they can close more business faster and more profitably.

OR, simply, **I help you sell more stuff!**

It all depends on how much I want to talk and how much time I think the person has to listen to what I have to say. I'd rather be asking them questions than boring them with my personal anecdotes. As I've said before, you sell things by listening, not talking.

Having moved and restarted my career and life a dozen times, I've become an expert in knowing what I need to do when I move to a new city or country where I know no one. You have to start connecting.

While I was shy and quiet until my twenties, thirties, ok until I was over 50, I learned that having a welcoming smile and asking questions about others was the easiest way to make new contacts and friends.

As I get older, I'm finding that I have to put myself out there more than I had to in my earlier years. I am better equipped emotionally and more open when seeking new friendships and relationships.

If Jane Fonda, in her 70s, can finally admit to her vulnerabilities on TV, then there's no reason for me not to open myself up in that same way. I believe that true intimacy only happens when you are open and honest and admit to those things that you'd prefer not to admit to.

The end result is that you are being your most authentic self and not someone who is terrified that you'll see through her perfect façade to the real person underneath. That had been my fear in the past.

Once I was able to acknowledge my strengths AND weaknesses, I became much more relaxed around people and accepting of their imperfections. I also finally stopped biting my nails in my forties.

In January 2010, I knew three people in Toronto—my semi-retired brother, my mother (who I hadn't spoke to in eight years), and my best friend from high school, a retired teacher. I had zero business contacts. I was starting two new businesses in my old hometown, a place I had never expected to live in again.

Now, seven years later, I know hundreds if not thousands of people who I've met through various groups, associations and networking events.

I made it a point to not only join associations like the Canadian Professional Speakers Association (CAPS) but to volunteer and get on the board. "Give to get" has always been one of my mottos.

The more you give to an association the more you'll get out of it. I've earned enough business as a result of being part of various associations to make any membership fees quite worthwhile. It's also a place to make new friends too.

Professional speakers are among the most interesting people around. They are well-travelled, know tons of interesting people, have amazing stories to share and are such positive people to be with.

I'm a connector. I introduce one person to another, helping them make more connections. If people tell me that it's hard to make friends in a new city, I know it's only based on the effort (or lack there of) that they've put into making new relationships.

Yes, you might need a bit of courage to go out and do things on your own, but what are the alternatives? Staying at home alone? That won't solve the problem of not knowing anyone in a new city. You get what you give, so you have to get out and get talking to get the contacts and friends that you want.

When I needed to meet new people in the city, I was ready to take advantage of everything it could offer me. That included a variety of activities like fitness, improv, social events, dating, dancing, dining and more. Business networking was a big part of it too as I desperately needed to get known in the business community of Toronto.

I exhausted myself that first year, taking classes, networking a few times a week, getting involved in different organizations, taking on volunteer roles and even getting back into dating. I was a Director on two Boards, taking on the Chair role for my alma mater Ryerson University's Business Alumni Association, as well as a business development role at CAPS.

My busy first year meant that my second year was all about consolidation and figuring out which connections were the most valuable and enjoyable to me, and which were not worth my time.

Since I went back to being a small business marketing consultant rather than a speaker's agent, that meant a new target market and new groups to join and learn about. Hustling once again!

When I started at CAPS Toronto, I didn't know anyone on the board. Before the year was over, I made a few new best friends and got acquainted with so many more people in the association, just from volunteering.

My volunteer work rewarded me in many ways, both professionally and personally. I was meeting amazing people, working and socializing with them. They helped me to recognize my own gifts and talents and to value them the way that they should be valued.

Relationships are so crucial in our lives. Even in the technology-driven world that we live in, you still sell, train, coach, consult and talk to one person at a time. It's still you interacting with that one other person. Whether that's in a business sales call or a spousal relationship, it comes down to people and how you treat each other.

The rules of sales have not changed, despite what anyone says on social media: **People still do business with people they know, like and trust.**

I say that you don't know if you're going in the right direction until you take the first step. Then you can decide if it's the right direction or not. Maybe you need to sidestep or even step back.

Back in Toronto, after that thirty-year detour, I took many steps and evaluated my progress. Was this what I wanted to do for the rest of my life? No? Okay, let's try again. I just kept moving until I found what I was meant to do. Me being me, it took many steps forward, backward, sideways and upside down to finally find where I was meant to be.

It seems like I never take the direct route when the detours are so scenic and full of life lessons. Just NEVER give up searching for what is right for you.

What can you do to get known when you enter a new market?

Join groups. There are hundreds of Meetup groups, all sorts of associations depending on interests, industry and specialization. Get involved. Don't just pay your dues, volunteer—that's how you get the most of any membership and get known (and becoming known is the first step to getting hired).

How can you get more comfortable talking to strangers?

Step out of your comfort rut. The more often you do it, the easier it gets. There is no shortcut to practice, practice and more practice. I used to be so nervous going into a room of strangers. It's hard to believe now but I was truly tongue-tied and almost mute.

Therapy also helped me get more self-aware, and the more comfortable I was with myself, the easier it was to reach out to others. Now I'm excited to meet new people every day and everywhere.

Be prepared with a few relevant questions when attending networking events or trade shows. Ask open-ended questions that might have nothing to do with what you do but everything to do with finding out more about this exciting new person. It's easy to get others to talk about themselves, so ask away.

You need to know your prospects before you can sell to them, so be curious and ask them what you would like to know. Some questions can include:

- Why did you come to this event?
- What have you seen that is exciting, new or interesting?
- What is your biggest challenge in your business?
- What is on your bucket list that is fun?
- What do you do in your spare time?
- What do you wish you had learned at school?
- When and where is your next holiday?

Networking should not be scary at all. People are only people and being Canadian, you know that we're nice and polite. But the people in the rest of the world are just as nice if you're nice to them. If you're in a foreign country, make a point of learning about their customs and how to say please, thank you and hello in their language.

Meeting people face-to-face is still the fastest way to grow your business if you're charging thousands of dollars per contract. It's harder to say no to someone's face than it is to ignore an email.

Take advantage of that, especially if you're shy, just if they want to work with you and then shut up and wait for them to answer. It usually is a YES!

PERSISTENT PATTI

....

THE POWER OF BEING PERSISTENT!

History has repeatedly shown how hundreds of highly
successful leaders (including ten Nobel prize win-
ners, dozens of best-selling authors and eight US
presidents) have either never graduated from college or university or, like me, were not always top scholars.

Getting top marks at school is no guarantee of success post-
school. Some people peak later in life—where it matters the
most!

Persistence is a word that has followed me around for most
of my life. It started in Grade ten, when it took three attempts
to successfully kick me out of my Catholic boarding school.
Luckily, I was the favourite of one nun, who went on bended
knee to Mother Superior each time I was to be expelled and
saved me.

That last time though, when I had broken every rule, and
even some that didn't exist yet (breaking into someone's suitcase
to steal a bottle of rum, hitchhiking to drink it with a couple

of guys and then lying about it surprisingly wasn't a rule just yet), they let me write my exams and go home for good.

The next time persistence came into play was when I tried to return to Ryerson University for my degree year. Their stipulation was that you have a "B" average in your third year. Of course, I had a "B" average in five out of six semesters, just not in that crucial fifth semester. I appealed and eventually they did let me in and I graduated on the Dean's Honour List (take that!).

The last school that tried to kick me out was York University, during the last semester of my MBA. The previous semester had been one of the worst times of my young life and I was only twenty-two. I had just broken up with my boyfriend, who was also doing his MBA and with whom I was writing my group thesis. As no one knew we were dating, no one could console me.

Business school in the 1970s was male dominated, about 85–90% male, so in order for me to be accepted as an equal and not as "the girlfriend", we kept our relationship secret. I had no money and had to work while taking six courses (more than the normal load of four or five courses).

On top of all that, I was having problems at home with my parents. Needless to say, I had no time or inclination to study much due to all this emotional stress and of course my grades suffered. Instead of having the required minimum 4.2 average, I had a 4.0 average. I was 70% finished my MBA and had a job at IBM that required me to complete it if I wanted that big salary increase.

Shortly after getting my report card in the mail, I got a letter expelling me from the school, even though I was already enrolled in the summer term. My tuition fees were refunded. To my horror, the cheque truly was in the mail.

It was time to panic, cry, plead, get down on my hands and knees and beg for them to consider my extenuating circumstances. After three weeks of agony, they let me back in and I graduated.

The moral here is that marks don't necessarily count in how successful your life will be post-school. From Dean's List to biz school reject in one year just showed me that if I took the time to study, I could do well.

Next up for Persistent Patti was when I was in IBM's Basic Systems Training program, where I was first taught how to sell. I was shy and quiet, not at all the chatty, bubbly person that I eventually became. I didn't do so well with the sales formula they taught as I didn't, and still don't, fit into your typical mould of what a salesperson should be.

It was only after I modified the skills that I had learned and made them fit my personal style, that I started enjoying sales. Where I always got bonus points, however, was for my persistence. I didn't give up easily even when perhaps I should have.

I barely scraped by through IBM's intensive two-week sales training, the pre-requisite to get into sales at IBM. However I made it and was asked to be part of an exceptional sales team, where I made a lot of money for my age. You don't always have to fit into the slot that people want you to fit into in order to succeed, even at big corporations. As long as you perform, you'll get paid and promoted as I was.

Being persistent is what allowed me to work in Europe. A lot of people say that they'd like to live and work overseas but they underestimate the stamina and patience it takes to be a landed immigrant. The rule to remember is that you are a guest in their country and have to follow their rules, even if you don't always agree with them.

Not following the rules when applying for my British work permit meant I had a six-month stint as an illegal immigrant. I had a German driver's license, a British car and a Canadian passport. Legally, I could only live in Canada, but in reality I juggled my life between England, Germany and Switzerland. What a life. Try keeping those stories straight.

So where does persistence come in as an entrepreneur? Like Churchill said, you must never ever ever give up, as you can be so close to success, especially when it looks the bleakest. When you are down to your last pennies and you really need your next prospect to pan out, you must find the inner strength and conviction to keep on trying.

Never give up hustling to make your business a success!

Always look for the opportunities that surround you—everywhere and everyday. 24/7, there is no off time when you're a startup entrepreneur. Opportunities surround you, if you look around and ask for what you want.

If you want the security of regular paycheques and holidays right from the start, having your own business might not be for you. It might be possible if you've got enough funds to buy a franchise, but it's still a lot of hard work to make it a success.

As the mutual funds prospectus states, "past performance is no guarantee of future results", so even owning a franchise operation comes with its own risks.

Network Marketing or Direct Sales (which used to be called Multi-Level-Marketing) is a good way to find out if you're up for the life of a hustler. As an entrepreneur, you'd better be up to the task or you're doomed to fail.

Network marketing will give you a proven system and the infrastructure for success, but you still have go out and find customers; they won't just come to you themselves!

The lesson to be learned is that persistence is essential for all entrepreneurs in order to survive and be successful. You do have to know when you're chasing a pipe dream and when to give up. If you're not able to sell a reasonable amount of your product or service within the first six months, it's time to re-evaluate your offering.

Do you have it priced right?

Is your target market correct?

Why are people not buying?

It's time to do some honest and open market research and reflect on your performance and objectives.

Are you spending enough time, energy and resources on sales and marketing?

You should be spending 80% of your time during the day and also going out at nights to networking events to further your reach.

Are you out meeting people or are you hiding behind a screen, playing on social media and hoping your posts go viral? Sorry, that's just not the way it happens.

Growing up in a family where my dad had his own business and where I learned to answer our home phone with his company name at a young age, it's not surprising that my siblings and I are all self-employed and have started our own businesses.

In order to make your dreams come true, you have to believe in yourself and get through those trying first years.

The realistic timeline for starting a business:

- In the first year—live on your savings and credit
- By the second year—break even
- Third year—start to make money
- Fourth and subsequent years—let the good times roll

Being in business for yourself is not for the faint of heart. It's for those who not trust in themselves but also trust that they have something to offer the world. They are the misfits who believe that they can change the world.

Entrepreneurs are those individuals who know that life will be better being their own bosses and who know how to work smarter not harder in order to succeed.

DON'T TELL ME WHAT TO DO!

PAYBACK IS SWEET

I was hired as the first female computer operator at IBM's Hamilton datacentre. All the other women employed there were data entry clerks (one step up from being a secretary). IBM did not treat me well the first time I worked for them as a naïve nineteen-year-old. I received no training whatsoever. Not one second in a classroom in the seventeen months that I worked for them, and this was a company whose employee training was deemed to be "world class". A paying customer bumped me from every course I was scheduled to attend.

By the time I finally got a confirmed seat in a class, I already knew how to operate three different mainframe computers so I never went. Despite my knowledge of different programming systems, I was considered "not qualified" to work as a programmer, as I didn't have a degree at the time and just a three-year diploma in Business Programming.

For my debut to operating IBM mainframe computers, they scheduled me for the Sunday midnight shift with a co-op student, who knew even less than I did (and I knew nothing). A senior operator scribbled some basic instructions on the back of a punch card and wished me luck.

He pointed to a ten-foot-wide array of technical manuals "in case anything goes wrong". I somehow managed to fumble my way through that first shift which really defined learning on the job.

The second time I worked for IBM, however, it was overkill on the education front. After six years of university, including grad school, where you're treated like you can walk on water, I was thrown back into what seemed like a high school classroom for six months of Basic Systems Training (BST). We learned about computers, business basics and how to sell, something that was never taught in biz school.

But I has remembered how they treated people without degrees and caught on to how they were trying to brainwash us to be their IBM clones. They wanted everyone to be part of the IBM family.—to dress the part, act the part and be completely loyal to the company for life. The HR representative talked to me about the gold watch that you got after twenty-five years of service and my eyes glazed over. Pensions? I was twenty three- years-old. Who cares about pensions at that age?

My real goal at IBM was to pay off my student debts, make a lot of money and move on. After only eighteen months, I managed to get myself on an excellent sales team with two other motivated women and we burned up our targets with a vengeance.

We were selling standard off-the-shelf software for mainframe computers for the first time in history and no one knew how to set realistic targets, so we made out like bandits.

However, it took a lot of energy to work at IBM. It was my first introduction to company politics, which made daily work life stressful. I only worked from 9-5 but felt like working 9-midnight as an entrepreneur. It was that stressful.

As I made the rounds saying my goodbyes after I'd finally had enough, many IBMers asked if I was moving to the competition, since I was seen as an up-and-coming go-getter. They were amazed and somewhat envious when I said I was actually taking time off to travel.

That was the first time I heard so many of my colleagues say, **"I wish I could do that"**, which made me wonder—**why don't you?**

Even though I decided to forget about IBM and move on, what I wouldn't ever forget was the way they had treated me...

Five years later I was in Germany helping my UK-based company sell £3,000,000 worth of IBM PC equipment. Since I knew all the PC resellers in Germany, it was natural for me to market to them. My dealers soon discovered that we were delivering computers faster and cheaper than IBM itself.

Customer testimonials are great for sales proof, so I took one customer's testimonial that we were "even better than IBM", pasted it on some promotional flyers and mailed them out to all of IBM's German dealers.

Through the grapevine via IBM Germany to IBM UK, I heard that they were not pleased with me and wanted me to stop saying we were better than them. With a twinkle in his eye, my boss' boss instructed me to "keep up the good work".

My revenge came soon after when a major PC dealer was disappointed with IBM Germany's inability to ship a certain interface board. They had been promised the board as part of a substantial order. Since we were the only IBM distributor to have them in stock, I knew IBM would reluctantly come crawling to negotiate with me.

I did what any good businessperson would do under the circumstances; **I sold IBM equipment back to IBM at a premium price including a surcharge.**

Hey, it's only business. How sweet it was! I am not usually one for payback, but the way they had treated me years ago had left a sour taste in my mouth. They tried to tell me what to do and say and that was not acceptable.

The moral of this story is: treat your staff, customers AND suppliers with respect and human decency. It has to be a **four-way win-win-win-win situation** for all involved or else the relationship is not sustainable. Don't expect your staff to learn on their own unless you're a small start-up company and they know in advance what is expected of them.

When you're a world-class corporation, you have an obligation to treat everyone with respect, no matter what their level of education is. I hated the fact that I was fawned over with my MBA but ignored with my lowly diploma. I was still the same person, so I should have been treated the same regardless.

A smart leader hires the best people no matter their nationality, skin colour, sexual orientation or gender. They hire to strengthen their weaknesses not to enlist a bunch of yes-men that will agree with whatever they say. You do not grow a company fast if only the boss has the best ideas and no one challenges him or her on them. Be the thorn in their side and the devil's advocate as that is the only way to point out blind spots and issues that might have been overlooked.

Don't work for ignorant leaders—pick the good ones who will treat you right. They're the ones to work for. Think enough of yourself to leave when the situation is not right for you and be confident that you will find a place that values your talents and will pay a fair market value for them.

There is no sense in being a victim; it's all a choice. Sometimes that choice is a difficult one, but without making difficult decisions, we'd never have any progress or growth in our lives.

The same goes for picking your clients. A huge perk of being your own boss is that you can choose who you want to work with. Yes, the money that large corporations can offer might be tempting but don't sell out just for the money.

To me, **life is too short to work anywhere you're not fully appreciated.** I'd rather borrow on my line of credit than go to work at a company that makes me hate my working life.

How are you treating people?

Do you differentiate between those who can do things for you and others who can't?

GUESS WHO I PISSED OFF?

....

IT NEVER HURTS TO BE NICE TO PEOPLE.
NICE SELLS!

After my initial year of traveling in Europe was up and I had decided to stay overseas, my IBM background ensured that I quickly found a position as Sales Manager at SM Software, a small start-up PC company, based in Munich.

They were surprisingly grateful that they could hire me, the ex-IBMer, and I was profoundly grateful that they hired me, the female foreigner who only spoke broken German.

My first few days on the job, whenever one of my bosses left my office, I'd quickly dig out my German-English dictionary to figure out what those words on the screen meant for the programs I was to be selling. There was a steep learning curve. I had to learn how to speak business German and familiarize myself with their customs.

I was headhunted for my second job in Germany at Sirius Computers by their American President because my English was so poor. Think about it, English is my native language but at that point I had become so immersed in German that I repeatedly stumbled while doing a demo of our software in English.

The President was so impressed with my fumbled demo that he made me an offer I could not refuse, more than doubling my salary and throwing in a bonus trip to California to their head office.

Sirius Computers was the leading PC company in Europe and manufacturer of the "Computer of the Year". We were the celebrity of the PC world in Europe. I was invited, along with my European HQ colleague Gerry, to the launch of a new PC software program and a newfangled tracking device for computers called a "mouse".

Remember, this was in the dark ages of personal computing. We still ran DOS, a non-graphical operating system on floppy disks (Google it if you don't know what I'm talking about).

At the launch I met the American president of this software company. He greeted me with a limp handshake and a total lack of interest. He was the typical skinny nerd with glasses, wearing a button-down shirt and Shetland wool sweater.

After a short introduction, we were allowed to look at the new software program and "mouse". Both Gerry and I are lefties, so the first thing we had to do was switch the device over to the left-hand side of the keyboard.

We tittered over the name, wondering why they had named it a mouse. It seemed unwieldy and awkward to use as it tested our hand-eye coordination, or lack thereof.

The software program was an English language word-processor, which obviously could not compete with the many German-language programs already established in the German-speaking world. Since I was responsible for the testing and quality of software for my 200 dealers, I went ahead and played with the program.

It was a beta, or pre-release, version of the software and not officially available yet. Anyone involved with software knows that pre-releases are subject to failures and crashes and this one was no exception.

Gerry and I continued to make fun of the new device, testing the software, and it wasn't long before I made it crash and stop working. I was an eclectic program tester and superb at finding the bugs or errors in any program. I still am the go-to person for finding bugs in a system. My mind just works differently than expected.

We hadn't noticed that the American president had been watching our antics, along with several of his major prospects that he was trying to impress. When the program inevitably crashed he gave me a dirty look and then rudely elbowed me aside to reboot the PC.

That was my first encounter with Bill Gates, the skinny nerd and head of Microsoft, when it was just another geeky start-up software company.

Everyone knows what happened to Microsoft. It had growing pains but succeeded despite bugs in their mediocre software and many complaints. With the focus, determination and confidence of its founders, it went on to become the standard operating system for personal computers and is still the world leader today.

Bill Gates obviously didn't let these little setbacks keep him down for long. At the same time, even having the "Computer of the Year" didn't keep the company that I worked for, Sirius Computers, alive after IBM's marketing clout made its impact. It was IBM after all and our computers were not IBM-compatible.

> The next time I saw Bill, was at a trendy Italian bistro in Chiswick, a non-touristy area of West London where I lived. My dining companion said, "how typical American. You can always hear them in a crowd!"
>
> I tipped my chair back to see the offender and said "Yes, and he's worth $400 million!" It was 1986. I was single and unemployed and didn't know whether to ask Bill Gates for a job or a date, as I had heard he liked smart blondes.
>
> He had beefed up considerably and gone for a more corporate look in a suit. I still wasn't attracted to him and I had no desire to work for his company. Pass.
>
> At least I know that I won't marry just for money.

Bill Gates wasn't the only person who treated others with disdain; Steve Jobs was notorious for yelling at his staff and demanding perfection. Doing this was not what made him and his company successful, it was his dedication to his business and his product that served as the foundation for the Apple empire.

Recently Amazon was in the NY Times where they interviewed 100 past and current Amazon employees, coming to the conclusion that Amazon was a horrible place to work. Their phone directory was frequently used to send secret feedback to bosses and ultimately sabotage one another.

That doesn't sound like a place anyone would want to work at. It sounds more like a reason to avoid being an employee at all and is similar to my own experience at my last corporate job before starting my own business in 1992.

Bill Gates could very well have achieved the same success he has today while still treating people with kindness. In retrospect, he probably didn't know that he had elbowed me out of the way that day, he was just that focused on demonstrating his product and could not handle anyone or anything that was delaying the process.

He gets bonus points for focus and dedication, but minus points for people skills. It all depends on what is important to you. He's now known for his philanthropy and I applaud that.

For me, it was important to take my time and have respect for people along the way. My experience of working in Germany taught me about being dedicated to success and staying true to your purpose, even though there might be some pitfalls along the way.

Celebrating victories are more meaningful when there are others to celebrate with you, instead of looking back at all the vanquished people along your path and being alone with your "success".

I attribute a lot of my personal success in sales and running different businesses to my outgoing and friendly personality. My clients don't think of me as a sales person but as someone they enjoy interacting with. I show them that I care more about meeting their needs rather than selling them a bill of goods that they did not need nor want.

There is never any need to hard sell anyone. A hard sell is a sign of a desperate person who doesn't know how to sell properly.

If after thirty-five years of selling, I've never had to resort to a hard sell, but have sold millions of dollars' worth of goods around the world, there's no need for you to be pushy about your product or service or to pressure someone to buy from you.

The only way to have a sustainable long-term business is to make sure you have way more fans, followers and clients than enemies—or even worse, resentful past clients! You cannot sell to everyone as you cannot click with everyone, but you do not have to piss people off on your way up the corporate ladder or when building a business.

So whether you are looking for a vendor or strategic partner or even when you're dating, observe people when they are interacting with wait staff. Are they just as nice and polite as they are to you or do they treat them as second or third class citizens?

As a previous waitress, I've experienced being treated subpar by others. I am not your servant; I am serving you, just like I do today when I get paid the big bucks to coach aspiring entrepreneurs. Treat others the way you want to treated, it's that simple.

Most of all, what I learned from my past experiences is that kind people can rise to top and sleep well at night, too. I'm proof of that! They can compete based on their capability and win because they have treated everyone with respect and decency. The race to finish first or be successful in business does not require an individual to sacrifice respect for other individuals, to abuse others along the way.

PASSION AND PROFITS

....

ARE YOU ONLY IN IT FOR THE MONEY?

Dave Rheaume, film director and editor, currently reinventing himself as an award- winning artist, says that of all the successful people he's interviewed, the one underlying thing that united them all was passion. Passion for what they did and what they stood for.

Without passion and purpose, you're only in it for the money.

Without passion, you have no overwhelming drive to succeed. Without passion, there is a discernible lack of enthusiasm. When people feel that you are only in it for the money, there is no authenticity in your communication. It's all about you, not them and they can sense it.

When you're trying to close a deal that is only really good for you and not the other party, it's not a sustainable business.

That's why it's so important to find a job, career or business that you feel passionate about. You can be passionate about the cause, the service or the product you offer others, knowing that you deliver real value and real benefits to others.

The way you can tell you're only working for a paycheque is if you're one of the TGIF bunch. Saying TGIF, Thank God It's Friday, means that you're wishing five days of your life away. Isn't that sad? If you feel totally burnt out by the end of the week and have nothing more to give, then you have to seriously look at your life.

There is no such thing as work/life balance. You only have one life, and you try and fit in as much as you can so you should do things that light you up, not burn you out. There is so much more to life than a paycheque and keeping up with the Facebook/Instagram crowd.

When it came to my reinvention as the owner of Down to Earth Gardens, all things flowers became my passion. I was obsessed with plants, with growing things, with understanding why people bought certain plants and how they grew. Everything I bought had a flower theme. I'd be up at 4:30AM some mornings, so excited to begin a new day. I was learning so much every day and it was physically and mentally challenging.

I relentlessly asked questions and fellow gardeners were gracious in offering up their experience and advice. I went from being a novice gardener to an expert. That is also when I finally lost my fear of public speaking.

Once you really know your topic and are passionate about it, people see that and relate to it. I acquired fans that asked me back to speak and my fears and nervousness faded away.

So, what would you do if money was not a problem?

That could be where your passions lie. Some experts tell you to go back to your childhood and see what used to get you excited. If I did that, I'd be a bank teller, teacher, vet or accountant—hardly anything that fills me with passion today. It depends on your childhood and how freely you dreamt back then and how well you knew yourself at an early age. Some of us are just late bloomers.

For me, it came when I realized that working for someone else was not the answer. They say that people leave managers and not companies and after working for many companies in several countries, I've had my share of bad bosses with a couple of exceptional ones too.

Passions do change. Many years ago I was passionate about working in Germany. It was part of my heritage. To learn to speak German and succeed in a new male- dominated world appealed to me. What I loved the most was being paid to travel and see the world.

Learning a new language in a different country was so exciting. It's what got me up every morning; I never knew what would happen and what I'd learn next.

It took me four years to conquer German and Germany, but having to change my bubbly personality and accept gender discrimination eventually had me fed up. and my passions shifted to England and everything British.

Passion ebbs and flows as life goes on. Dogs remain a constant passion of mine. I've had a number of fur babies in my life having gone only two days without one in almost thirty years! Those two days, I cried non-stop and I hitched up our llamas and took them for a walk. I was inconsolable until I got the next dog and magically stopped crying.

I was once "that Llama Lady of Burritt's Rapids"; that "Down to Earth flower lady"; and "the barcode expert"— goes to show the lengths I'll go to in order to not be bored in life. Today, my new passion is helping entrepreneurs grow their business; sharing my hard-won sales experience and knowledge so that they can sell more.

One of my taglines as a small business marketing consultant is "I help you make your passion profitable with my proven practical advice!" And I truly am passionate about your business making money.

A business is only a hobby UNLESS it makes money!

That is the main difference between doing what you love and making a business out of what you love. Many boomers have finally cast off their golden handcuffs that were keeping them tied to a miserable (or sometimes delightful) corporate job and are now free to reinvent themselves.

Some of them are taking their long-pursued hobby and seeking to make some money from it. Others are looking at franchises or finally opening long dreamt of businesses.

Money is also the currency of worth for boomers. It is somehow tied to our self-worth and self-esteem too. We were raised to save money for later in life. **Now is later.** It is finally time to spend some of your hard-earned money and enjoy life more. You can't enjoy it when you're dead or in such bad health that you can't go many places. **Enjoy your wealth while you have your health!**

Taking a hobby from a pleasurable time-suck to a money-generating activity means understanding how a business works.

You need to know:

- if you need liability insurance,
- whether you should be incorporated or not;
- how to understand cash flow, especially if you're into manufactured products.

Do you need employees and all the paperwork that the government requires for that?

How will you get the word out and market your new business in order to make some sales?

What kind of training or coaching will you need?

What government resources are out there to help you?

Think carefully about what you wish for too. Having had the pressure of twenty people's mortgages on my shoulders was a stressful time in my past that I never want to have again in my life. I prefer to contract out what I need when I need it. No more employees for me.

Brian Tracy, a noted speaker and author, was asked what regrets he had in his business and he said it was growing too big. Now he has to work in order to keep his huge operations going. There are times when small is beautiful. Having freedom from bureaucracy and managing other people can be a wonderful thing.

So be careful what you wish for, nothing comes without a price.

Remember, without passion there is no real purpose in what you do. Passion is what gets you up in the morning. It's what keeps you alive and vital no matter what your age is telling you. If you do not love what you do, CHANGE something!

Life is too short to not be living as fully as you can.

When people who are dying are asked what they regret most, it's the things that they DID NOT do that they regret the most. The chances that they did not take are what they regret not doing. The dreams that they left behind, unfulfilled, more regrets.

So what dreams have you not fulfilled?

What would you regret not having done by the time you're too old to do anything about it?

What's stopping you from living your dream?

Do you say TGIF, which means you're wishing 5 out of 7 days of your life away?

What would it take to say TGIM – Thank God It's Monday and I get to work again!

Figure out what is stopping you and start living. Yes, it's not safe, it's not comfortable BUT it is living and eventually it will be safe and comfortable again and you'll be so much happier having accomplished what you have always dreamt about.

LIFE IS TOO SHORT—DON'T BE THE WORKING DEAD

LIVE ON THE EDGE!

"Have fun and make money" has been my personal and business motto for twenty-five years now (Thanks J.R., I know I borrowed it from you).

I know the difference between leaping out of bed excited for the day to begin and sleeping through my alarms and dragging my butt around the whole day.

Several jobs have taught me that life is too short to waste on energy-sucking positions. The first time I experienced this was a summer job at an insurance company where I was determined to stick it out.

I'm not sure why I decided I had to stay, but once I had made that decision, I stubbornly stuck to it. (I am a Taurus on the cusp of Gemini, which makes me double stubborn.)

What a mistake! They thought I was a great worker and wanted me to quit school and work for them fulltime. Picture

The Scream by Edvard Munch, that's what I felt like. It was boring, monotonous work and I was surrounded by people who didn't challenge or interest me.

After that, I promised myself that I would never again feel forced to stay in a job that was not bringing joy to my life. It's just not worth it. I would recommend that you take the risk that something better is out there instead of playing it safe. That advice works for relationships too. Life is not meant to be miserable.

It goes to show that at times you should re-evaluate previous decisions and never feel like you have to stick to something just because you said you would. Just because we have promised something and made a commitment doesn't always mean that we can never change our minds.

This doesn't give you the right to stop doing something you committed to because it's not as much fun as you thought it would be.

There's a definite distinction between making yourself miserable for eight hours a day, five days a week, for years on end and doing something occasionally that you don't really enjoy.

After four years of working in Germany, something I was originally very passionate about, I was getting frustrated with gender discrimination. Being in a meeting and having someone repeatedly say to my face, "isn't there a MAN I can talk to?" or being ignored because there was a male present got old very quickly.

There isn't anything more infuriating than a female secretary asking, "which MAN are you calling on behalf of?" With my barely concealed rage, I would snarl out, "I'm returning his call to ME! Please put me through!"

I had to learn how to be snarky in order to get ahead, something that didn't come naturally to me. My personality had to change in order for me to succeed.

As a guest in their country, I couldn't do much more to change their attitudes than I already was simply by being a successful businesswoman. I had quadrupled my starting salary within three years, making as much as doctors and dentists.

It would take another twenty years for females to finally gain more equality in the business world and I didn't have the patience to wait it out, so it was up to me to change, and this meant leaving Germany.

Not quite ready to return to Canada, I moved to England. My one-year of travel had already taken five years and my European adventures continued.

The next time I realized that my best-before date had arrived was at a company where I had worked for five years. There had been a change in leadership and after firing an underperforming sales rep, my new boss said there was no need for a fulltime sales manager and I was demoted .

I had that horrible dual-role of sales manager AND sales person where I had personal AND team targets, a sales team to manage as well as my own major accounts. Talk about conflicting priorities!

Sell or manage… it's horrible because you end up doing two jobs poorly instead of one really well.

I was asked to vacate my office, a petty move on their part. I didn't deserve that kind of treatment. I had been one of the company's sales superstars in England and in Canada where I had tripled my department's sales the previous year.

Once I got my tax refund that would allow me to pay my expenses for a few months, I was out of there. I took some time off over the summer, volunteering as a sales rep at my boyfriend's start-up business (which eventually became Sage Data Solutions, the barcode company) and took my time figuring out my next move.

....

For my final gig as an employee, I was working at one of the world's largest computer companies where I lasted seven months. I had one customer, Canada Post, recognized as one of the top toxic companies to work for.

I had to chair large meetings where they slung verbal tomatoes at each other while I tried to stay out of firing range. It was beyond bad from both a customer and employee standpoint.

Nothing in life is worse than watching the clock to see when you can finally go home. Life is way too short to live that way. How many people do you know that are ticking down the days until they can retire?

Selling to the federal government for years, I would notice some cubicle-dwellers with a five to ten-year retirement schedule that they were marking off, day by day by long day.

Can you imagine crossing out 11 years, 2 months and 20 days—day-by-day-by day? What do you think those cubicle dwellers really felt like inside? To hate each and every moment that they spent "working", how sad is that?

Life is way too short to be in a place that is not fulfilling you most of the time. If you go to work and are counting down the hours/minutes/days to the end, that is so wrong on so many levels.

It can be changed to a life of daily joy and happiness that you pass on to everyone you meet. It's a simple solution but hard to do. You do have to make plans on how you escape out of your toxic environment, as life is truly too short to waste.

A good indicator for your current situation is how you feel at the end of a workweek. Are you exhausted or are you gently and happily tired with a sense of accomplishment, certain that you've done something meaningful?

That is the difference between running a marathon you trained for and are excited to do vs. running a marathon that someone else is forcing you to run.

Where have you been treading water or living cautiously?

Have you been noticing more aches, pains and fatigue, like you're beat at the end of the week and need time off?

My despised jobs have led me to my philosophy that life is way too short to be in a place that is not fulfilling you most of the time. Let's be realistic—you're not going to get 100% joy anywhere but it should be at least 80% of the time.

If you go to work and are counting down the hours to the end, whether that end be the next break or the end of the day or when you can retire…

PLEASE DO NOT DO THIS!

Too many people have stayed the course, being too afraid to get out of their comfort ruts. They put all their hopes on that distant day when they turn 60-65 and can retire with a full pension. So when that day does arrive—then what?

They have spent so many years just surviving until they can get their pension that they haven't thought about what kind of life they want to have once they no longer have a hated workplace to go to. Now what?

Sadly, and all too frequently, they are the ones who retire and die way too soon after leaving their toxic environments. These places consume your best parts, literally sucking the life out of you so that when you finally leave, you have lost your purpose in life. You're gone without having lived your life to the best it can be.

You carry an aura of doom and gloom with you as you see life as something to be endured rather than enjoyed. I observe this on those rare occasions when I commute during rush hour on public transport. There are people on board hating their lives and end up taking it out on innocent bystanders.

Running my own business, I translated my "do not work for toxic companies" motto into "do not take on toxic clients". These are people who have wasted so much of my time that they've made my list of customers I choose not to deal with.

In the same way that there are toxic clients in our lives, we also have friends or family who are energy givers or energy suckers. If you feel depleted after spending time with someone, then it's time to reassess your relationship with them. I truly believe that people and relationships are there for a reason, season or a lifetime.

Even when you think it's a lifetime, it can be time to cut a friendship or relationship off or adjust how much time you spend with someone. It's a hard thing to do, to let go of a long-term relationship, but that only means that you're creating an opening for new and stronger relationships.

Not leaving a toxic work environment or friendship can have major negative impacts on your life. Not only will it sap your energy and leave you with physical and mental health issues due to stress but you'll be less engaged in life and you'll become an energy-sucker rather than a positive life force. Most likely, you'll stop respecting yourself when you avoid dealing with these uncomfortable situations.

Enjoying your passions and hobbies, such as physical exercise, is one great way to get rid of stress and feel more energetic. My time on the farm showed me the benefits of being fit and able to do anything physical that I wanted to.

Physical exercise releases nature's drug, endorphins, and makes you feel good. So even if you have to put up with a toxic work place, it can make it more tolerable.

Should you find yourself in a bad work environment, and this can creep up on you, it's time again for that dreaded "p" word—the Plan.

How do you get yourself out of that situation? Not everyone can just leave their job without having another source of income, that's where the plan comes in.

Figure out what money you have to earn in order to survive and pay the bills. What can you cut out of your life, like perhaps the luxury holidays you think you need in order to deal with your toxic workplace. If your workplace is no longer toxic, then maybe a more modest holiday will do so you need less money .

Decide in exquisite detail exactly where you want to go, what kind of employer you want, the kind of work you want to do and for whom and then go for it!

If you do take the risk and leave that soul-destroying environment, you have the potential to be happier, more energetic, have fewer health issues and set a good example for those around you, like your partner and kids.

So when you think things can't get any worse and that you've bottomed out, you're right. At some point, you need to call it a day and get out of the mess that you've gotten yourself into.

I once had three properties with six mortgages in three countries—talk about stress. But I made a plan and slowly got myself out of that financial mess that was keeping me tied to my employer, until I was able to resign on my own terms.

My old business partner used to say, "don't come to me with problems, come to me with solutions". That's why it doesn't help to blame anyone but yourself for the mess you are in.

Remember that by pointing a finger at someone else, there are three fingers pointing back at YOU. You're the only one who can change your circumstances.

The less energy you spend on bemoaning your fate, the more time you can spend proactively doing something about it. Action towards the goals and outcomes you want is the only thing that matters.

Life is too short to not be as happy as you can be!

What are you settling for in your life?

This is not a dress rehearsal,

This is YOUR LIFE!

LIVE IT!

BEING UNSTOPPABLE

....

NEVER EVER GIVE UP ON YOUR DREAMS!

I f you were following someone's directions, ignoring your GPS, and came to this barrier and sign, what would you do?

At first, I was taken aback. I stopped my car and took a moment to think about it. Hmmm, my friend didn't tell me about this but she had said that she lived on an old Air Force base. Maybe it's a leftover sign? Maybe I am technically authorized since I am going to visit with her permission (funny, how we can rationalize anything in our minds).

I drove past the barrier and followed the path, which got narrower and narrower, until it ended in a footpath and I could drive no further. There wasn't a soul or a house to be seen.

I returned to the main street and now looking at my GPS, it did say, go another 150 yards… I truly have no sense of distance and constantly turn at the wrong street, before I should. Following my GPS now, I turned at the next street, and that's when her directions made sense. I saw the new houses, I passed the day care and I found her house. It was the second street on the left, not the first! She assumed that the first street didn't count because of the barrier.

She had underestimated the power of Persistent Patti. NOTHING gets in my way once I get started on something. My powers of concentration can be quite incredible. The house can explode and fall down around me and I wouldn't notice if I'm working on something that has captivated me.

It used to drive my ex-partner insane. Too bad. It's a really great trait to have when stuff needs to get done, no matter where I am or how busy it is in the background, I just focus on the task at hand. Everything else is filtered out and ignored.

As we're coming to the end of this book and the result of a 60+ year journey so far, I'm excited about what's coming next. I say that nothing that I do surprises me anymore.

The message I want to leave you with is to **be UNSTOPPABLE!** That's what that sign was telling me. Don't let anyone or anything stop you when you're doing what you are meant to be doing.

Following your purpose, your passion, your calling, your goal in life is usually not easy. It eventually becomes easier once you master what it is you want to become. Going from beginner to expert takes time and you have to experience a few valuable life and business lessons along the way. And those lessons tend to hurt and be expensive.

The journey is not a straight line either. If it were, it would be boring and come too easy. That is one reason I left Toronto it the first place. Life had seemed to be easy for me. Yes, I worked hard and I achieved a lot but I still didn't feel good enough.

I didn't feel like I deserved my hard-earned recognition. I was scared of being a leader but deep inside of me, I knew I was one. It was buried very deeply and only has emerged in the last decade.

I wanted to challenge myself with things that were extremely tough, The life of an entrepreneur can be gruelling and can put a strain on your determination. At times it will make you question your sanity. Being an entrepreneur is not for the faint of heart.

You have to believe in what you're doing 200%; know that you're here to change the world in some way. That you'll make the world better with whatever it is that you're passionate about.

There's this saying that I love and believe:

> Entrepreneurship is living a
> few years of your life like most
> people will not,
> so that you can spend the rest
> of your life like most people
> cannot!

The first years of running your own business ARE tough. You'll be living on credit or savings and you'll find that they deplete faster than you ever imagined they could. Sales take much longer to close and at much smaller amounts and for much less profit.

Your business plan might start to look more like a fiction novel than reality. But you can never give up hope. You have to get up each day and think: this is the day it all changes! This is the day it turns around. This is the day you land that first big client. And eventually that day will happen. You'll look back and see some significant turning point.

You zigged, you zagged, you pivoted but finally you landed where you were meant to be. Restarting my life after my 30-year detour back to my hometown of Toronto, I started six businesses in five years until I found where I was meant to be.

It's not like buying a car, where I know as soon as I sit in it if it's for me or not. In business, it takes longer to figure out. As you may have guessed, I'm not one to stay too long where

I'm not feeling fulfilled. If I cannot get up in the morning and be energized by the day ahead, something is not right and it's my responsibility to make it right.

Be unstoppable in your business. Be so committed to what you do and the problems you solve that you make it work. No matter what. It might take some eighteen-hour days, seven days a week for a while, but you will succeed if you have truly identified a market that needs what you provide.

Being your own boss has pros and cons. In the short term, more cons than pros. No pain no gain is not just for the gym but for entrepreneurs too. You have to be able to power through the early stages, when you and everyone around you doubt that you will be successful.

You have to ignore the naysayers and only listen to the fire in your belly. Visualize the final outcome—whatever that means to you. If it's millions in the bank, running a huge company with hundreds of employees, selling a company for millions of dollars, being front page news, being on TV, being known by only one name, winning a prize or awards. **Whatever huge wild success looks like to you—never let it out of your mind.** Keep it in the back of your mind always. Have photos like a vision board or reminders of where you want to go.

Your WHY drives your HOW and keeps you doing what you MUST do in order to survive, then thrive, then feast on the victory. And victory is sweet.

Life is great. You make it great.
Never stop having dreams to go after.
Dream BIG and JUST DO IT!

ACKNOWLEDGEMENTS

....

This book was made possible by CAPS— the Canadian Association of Professional Speakers. While I was on the board, I ran a series of Book Writing Boot Camps led by the talented and ever so patient Book Coach and Ghost Writer Les Kletke.

To keep the momentum going, we initiated weekly book writing club calls. Thank you to Les Kletke, Sylvia Plester-Silk, Michelle Ray, Carol Ring, Janet Rousse (also my amazing book cover designer) and Jennifer Spear. Without you, this book would not have happened.

Thanks to Simon T. Bailey who introduced me to my OBO, (Oh Brilliant One) Helen Wilkie, who became my accountability partner and speaking mentor. Without her encouragement, I wouldn't be a small business coach, which is where my passion lies, in watching people and companies grow.

Finally, my brilliant and devoted editor Claire Pokorchak kept me to some sort of schedule with her gentle reminders. Again with her, no book.

To my friends and family who have kept me alive with love

and support during all my adventures – thank you. Knowing you were there for me is what kept me going during the lonely and fun times.

My thanks to the great team at Sage Data Solutions, lead by President John Rivenell (and run by Doreen Wallace lol), where we had so much fun, and now in it's 26th year.

"Have fun and make money" really does reflect my attitude about work and life. Even Dave Chilton (better known as The Wealthy Barber), confirms that this is the right order of things.

If you're not having fun, then who cares about the money.

And the more fun you have—the more money you'll make!

My hope for you, after reading this book, is that you'll come up with your own wacky ideas that work!

Have fun. Make Money. Repeat.

Have a great life.

PATTI POKORCHAK, MBA

....

Patti is an award winning marketing and sales executive, with 30+ years of experience at IBM and many start-up companies. Self-employed since 1992, she helped start and run a 7-figure 20 employee software company for 10 years before opening a thriving garden centre and hobby farm.

Patti was NOT a born salesperson. She was a trained programmer, and was shy, introverted and nervous. Making six-figures by the time she was 25, she decided that there had to be more to life than climbing the corporate ladder.

Wanting to live a life with no regrets, she left for a year of travel in Europe and returned nine years later. Finally, after a 30-year detour, she returned to her hometown of Toronto, Canada.

Patti says "If I can be a farmer, then you can be anything you want to be — as long as you have some basic sales and marketing skills that is!"

She loves to help make your passion profitable with her proven practical advice.

Contact Patti at Patti@SmallBizSalesCoach.ca or via her website at SmallBizSalesCoach.ca

Twitter @SmallBizSalesCo

She can help grow your business and take you from Sales FEAR to Sales FUN!